The Hermit of Africville

The Life of Eddie Carvery

Jon Tattrie

Pottersfield Press, Lawrencetown Beach, Nova Scotia, Canada

Library and Archives Canada Cataloguing in Publication

Tattrie, Jon
The hermit of Africville : the life of Eddie Carvery / Jon Tattrie.

ISBN 978-1-897426-18-0

1. Carvery, Eddie. 2. Africville (Halifax, N.S.)--Biography.
3. Black Canadians--Nova Scotia--Halifax--Biography. I. Title.

FC2346.26.C37T38 2010 971.6'225 C2010-902389-7

Cover design by Gail LeBlanc
Front cover and photos of Eddie Carvery on pages 7 and 193 by Darrell Oake
Photo of Victor Carvery on page 148 by Jon Tattrie
Author photo on back cover by Giselle Melanson
Jon Tattrie's website: www.jontattrie.ca

Pottersfield Press acknowledges the financial support of the Government of Canada through the Book Publishing Industry Development Program for our publishing activities. We also acknowledge the ongoing support of the Canada Council for the Arts, which last year invested $20.1 million in writing and publishing throughout Canada. We also thank the Province of Nova Scotia for its support through the Department of Tourism, Culture and Heritage.

Pottersfield Press
83 Leslie Road
East Lawrencetown, Nova Scotia, Canada, B2Z 1P8
Website: www.pottersfieldpress.com
To order, phone toll-free 1-800-NIMBUS9 (1-800-646-2879)
Printed in Canada

Canada

The Canada Council for the Arts Le Conseil des Arts du Canada

NOVA SCOTIA
Tourism, Culture and Heritage

1

The packed meeting at the Halifax North Memorial Library was tense. People were angry. It had been thirty years since the City bulldozed their homes and feelings were as raw as burnt skin. Eddie Carvery listened, then took his turn at the microphone.

The mayor was there. The city manager, too, plus the media.

It was August 1994. Eddie was a teenager when Africville came down in the 1960s. He was in his forties now, bushy goatee jumping out of his chin, wavy black-and-grey Einstein hair shooting out of the back of his head, a bright African shirt wrapped around his barrel chest. He started talking about the murder of Africville, Nova Scotia.

"We were never compensated," he said, voice rising. "We're still fighting."

All the homes that the City of Halifax demolished in the 1960s, they could have been fixed up, he said. Africville people could still be living in them. All the new houses that had sprouted up on the land of Africville in the last three decades could have belonged to Africvillians.

"We've got nothing. We could've had our homes, but they decided we weren't worth a home for a home. They decided they would take our homes and put a dog dung park there, and that's what they did. There's enough room in Africville that we didn't have to have our community blazed. We could've had new homes and we still could have our community today. There's enough space for everybody!" Eddie shouted. His face was passionate as his voice ramped up like a preacher's.

"It didn't just happen to me. It happened to all of us," he cried. Dispossessed Africvillians cheered, shouted Amens. The mayor stared straight ahead. Reporters took notes.

Martin Luther King III had come to Africville in February 1992. Camera flashes popped and politicians grinned as the son of the civil rights legend broke soil on the battered earth burying Africville. The church was to be rebuilt. The church the City had smashed to pieces in the middle of the night three decades earlier, breaking the spirit of the final resistance. After that, the trickle became a torrent as Africvillians evacuated their community, throwing their belongings on the back of the yellow dump trucks borrowed for the move to temporary housing in the city. Their homes were bulldozed behind them.

The rebuilt church would be the City's gesture of peace, an effort to heal old wounds, a symbol of Africville's undying soul, the world was told.

But the broken soil was all that remained of the latest broken promise. There was no church in Africville. There was no nothing. Just Eddie, as always.

Eddie opened his mouth to speak again.

"You're a bunch of welfare bums," a voice interrupted from the back. Eddie paused, but continued speaking.

"You don't deserve nothing," the intruder shouted.

Eddie stopped talking, turned to face his heckler. He was a Black man, a little younger than Eddie. Eddie knew him. He wasn't from Africville. He laughed at Eddie.

"They did you guys a favour. You were out there in Africville, living off the dump and you never had nothing," he sneered. All eyes flitted between Eddie and the heckler. Photographers raised their cameras and reporters turned on their recorders.

Eddie stopped talking, started walking.

"Excuse me," he snarled as he prowled, his old street temper flaring. "Excuse me!"

The big, belligerent intruder grinned. The grin died when he got a better look at Eddie's face.

"Not in here, Eddie," he said, backing up, hands up. The library was packed and the big man couldn't move quickly.

Eddie stormed to the six-footer, glaring up from his five foot eight.

"Take it easy," the big man said.

Eddie threw a wild right, missed, threw a wild left, missed, and then levelled the heckler with a monster right hook that smacked him straight under his jaw, slamming his mouth shut. Cameras popped like it was Ali vs. Fraser as the heckler toppled over backwards. Women screamed, men leapt from their chairs. A group grabbed Eddie and hauled him backwards while others dragged the cursing intruder out of the meeting room. The mayor jumped up and retreated, looking for help.

The bleeding heckler was heaved out of the library. Eddie patted down his shirt, rubbed his fist. Walked back to the microphone.

"Look guys, excuse me for this disruption," he said to nervous laughter. "This is an important meeting. You say one day we're going to put a replica church up there, and everyone's going to be happy because of everything you did for us. You did shit for us. There is such a thing as civil disobedience. That Fairview container pier is on our land and so is the MacKay Bridge. I don't think you guys would like it very much if seven o'clock Monday morning, we decided to start walking back and forth in front of it and just stop traffic for a couple of hours. You're not listening to us and you're not taking us seriously, and I hope we don't have to resort to nothing like making the people suffer for your mistakes. Deal fair with us."

The audience called out and clapped. Some shook their heads, outraged by the violence. Everyone knew Crazy Eddie. Sure, it was good Africville had a voice, a last living resident, a thirty-year protester, but did it have to be him? The one-time speed freak and crack addict jailed for beating a woman?

They had all left their homes decades before, chased by the bulldozers and pulled by the promise of a better life. The last Africvillian had left in 1970. Everyone thought it was over.

It wasn't over.

Eddie Carvery still lived in the buried graveyard of his childhood. Before the last Africvillian left, Eddie was there, sleeping rough, sleeping in borrowed spaces, sleeping in tents and campers, transforming from a low-level crook, drug addict and wife-beater into the world's most stubborn political protester, a poor man's Nelson Mandela taking a long walk to an uncertain future with no one holding candles outside his prison door.

Eddie wasn't born to be evicted from his home, to flee west and wind up in prison, to come home to find his world demolished. He wasn't born to be called "nigger," to be shot at, to see his family firebombed, to take a life, to try to take his own life, to suffer seven heart attacks while living a hermit's existence in the frozen fields of empty Africville and be run off his land in a nightmarishly repeating cycle of urban renewal. He wasn't born to wander forty years alone through a wilderness like an abandoned Moses.

But there he stood, the Last Africvillian, the Hundingo Man, as he named himself, a broken body defeated by everything except one thing: building a spiritual Africville out of desolate lands.

The meeting came to a close. Promises were made. Everybody went home. Eddie went back to Africville.

2

Edward Leo Carvery was born in Africville on October 5, 1946, eased from his mother Daisy's womb into the world by his grandmother, Hattie Carvery, better known as Granny Pink, in his parents' bedroom. It was a difficult birth, but he survived, unlike a brother before him and a sister after.

Granny Pink noticed something very unusual about the child as soon as he entered the world.

"He's got the veil," she whispered.

The veil, the caul: a mask that covers the rare child's head at birth. The veil is a good luck charm, an indicator of second sight. Eddie, a caul-bearer, would see things that weren't there.

They called him Edward, which means blessed guard.

They called him Leo, which means the lion.

Granny Pink removed the veil carefully, setting it aside, handing the bronze baby to Daisy. Exhausted, she smiled at her curly-haired boy.

"It's the caul," whispered her mother. "It's a good omen."

Daisy held the crying baby, comforting the far-seeing boy.

3

The Carvery household was a big one packed into five rooms. All the kids slept in one bedroom while Daisy and Clarence lived in the other. When he was home, anyway. Clarence had a lot of jobs, and a bad temper. He worked as a truck driver for the coal companies, as a stevedore on the nearby docks and at the slaughterhouse for a spell before he landed a job with the merchant marine. He wasn't home much after that. That wasn't a big problem for his family.

Houses in Africville grew up the hill like a field of wild flowers. Everyone painted and designed their home according to their own taste. Maybe that was why the city folk called it the coloured part of town. The village stretched out to the shimmering, circling shelter of the blue-watered Bedford Basin and its tree-lined hills.

Eddie and his family lived in Miss MacDonald's house. There were two houses on the property, theirs and Miss MacDonald's. The land ran from the dirt road right back to the shore. Behind the house was a big field with an apple tree. Eddie and his brothers and sisters, cousins and friends spent endless hours out there, swimming in the Basin, playing on the field, or just lying down and staring at the clouds passing through the untroubled skies overhead.

Down the road was Joe Skinner, who got the first artesian well in Africville. That meant it was dug deep into the rocky land and you hardly had to pump it at all. You still had to boil the water, of course. There were signs everywhere telling you that. Eddie's family got its water from Mr. Skinner's well.

Next was Aunt Tilly. She had a little store and kept turkeys, along with the nastiest geese in Canada. They were worse than guard dogs. The ill-tempered birds snapped at anyone who came too close. She married a West Indian man called Red Newman. He became a good friend to Eddie. Eddie later worked the dump with Red's son, his cousin Mannie.

Up the road, Jack Carvery's house bustled with his big family. Just when everyone thought they were done, they somehow found room for his wife's sister's kid.

Eddie was alive in Africville for two years before word reached up over the hill and down into the City of Halifax. When his brother Victor was born, his parents decided it was time to register two births in one trip and made the journey to where the dirt road grew pavement on Barrington Street and the city began.

There were always babies in the house. First the children, then the children's children, plus a mix of family and friends staying a while. Usually, in Africville, when a family expanded too much for one house, they built another one next door. There were always electricians, carpenters and stone masons in Africville who learned their trades from their parents, so people saved up, paid cash and got a new home built. Who got a permit? Nobody. Who could even get a permit? Nobody. Tax-paying people, Africvillians rendered unto Caesar what he wanted, but Caesar didn't render much back to them. No sewage, no running water, no paved roads. And no permits.

But never mind that for now. Eddie was born into a bustling house. Babies, older siblings, parents, and the old man, Uncle Sonny, who wasn't actually anybody's uncle. Eddie was never sure how Uncle Sonny had come to live with them, but there he was.

It got even more bustling when Bill Gannon's house burned down. He, his wife and their kids managed to escape, but the house was a goner. The City fire department eventually found its way to Africville and spat a little water on the smoking ruins.

Uncle Bill and his family were out of a house, but not homeless. The Carverys had not only a kitchen and a living room, but a whole extra back kitchen that had been added onto the house. The fire had barely cooled off when the family moved in to stay with the Carverys for a couple of years.

"It was space, and they needed a place," as Eddie's mother explained it.

Eddie was never entirely clear on who lived in his house, but the Gannons joined his sisters Evelyn, Snookie and Priscilla, his brothers Milton (who died young of pneumonia), Raymond, Clarence (everyone called him Dickie), Victor and Irvine. Daisy had twins, too, but they died in infancy due to the conditions in Africville. Raymond was Eddie's oldest brother and people said he looked just like him. That made Eddie feel mighty proud. Raymond was Eddie's hero and he carried Eddie everywhere on his back. The brothers would run to the field on piggyback, where Raymond would read Eddie funny books. The two were always goofing off.

When Daisy was working for the rich white people, Evelyn stepped in to do the raising. Daisy worked at the hospital's cleaning department and later the kitchen. The kitchen was a great job, as far as Eddie was concerned, because she brought home all kinds of goodies – including real butter! For a while there, Eddie had butter every night with his bread or vegetables and felt like the most decadent prince in the world. Daisy moved on to a job at the Nova Scotia Hotel, though, and the butter supply dried up.

Evelyn started her own family the same time as Eddie's younger brother Irvine was born. Evelyn had her second child when Daisy gave birth to Priscilla. That was it for Eddie's mom, but Evelyn still had a bunch of kids in front of her.

4

When the house got too chaotic, or his father was in a particularly foul mood, Eddie went to his secret hiding spot. He was only five, but he had discovered it watching his dog Dusty one day. Dusty had been hanging out in front of the house, watching people coming and going, watching the steady stream of visitors to his grandmother's post office down the road, when a train came flying through Africville and she fled under the house. Eddie wondered where she'd gotten to.

Ever since the City had first built train tracks cutting through Africville in the 1850s, knocking down some nice houses on the way, trains came storming through the village without warning. The monstrous, lethal machines screamed past at all hours, shaking houses, knocking dishes to the floor and occasionally running someone over. At nighttime, no matter how bad a nightmare you were having, you'd wish it would go on, rather than having to wake to the dark energy surging along the lines. The black smoke was awful.

Victor had seen a white man's body on the tracks once. He was walking out of a shop early one morning and there it was: a corpse, crushed on the tracks. Victor ran back inside the shop. The shop owner came out and covered the body with a sheet. Eventually, someone from the City came to claim it. The white man had come to Africville for the cheap alcohol, drank too much and passed out on the tracks. The train didn't see him. It didn't stop, either, so maybe the driver didn't even notice when he killed the sleeping man.

As Eddie wondered where Dusty had gone, a squad of Africvillians stood silently watching the Dominion Coal train from Sydney creak and groan through the village. It was moving slow, heading for the yard just beyond Africville. A few men were way ahead, waiting for the signal. The rest of the team – boys, men, women – waited by its passing side. Coal glittered in the sun on top of the open hoppers.

The advance members jumped onto the side of the moving train and scaled it silently. With a nod to the men below, they started bagging and tossing coal to land.

When the train's front car reached the end of the village, a nod set off phase two. The men far ahead pulled the air brakes. With a loud, dying groan, the train stopped. Twelve of the raiders stormed the train, throwing loose coal to waiting hands below while the conductor restarted the train.

Eddie ran across the tracks to grab a piece of the action. It was fall and the house was freezing at night. There wasn't a scrap of coal left in Africville.

"Don't touch the coal that the boys throw off the hoppers," his mother warned him from the house as he slipped under the train. Eddie dropped the piece in his hand. "Wait till they're finished and then you take the bucket and pick up the little pieces."

Eddie sulked, but obeyed. The older men got the lion's share, bent double under the weight of the coal bags. Eddie grabbed a bucket and ran behind them, snatching up the loose pieces as they fell.

A lot of Africville men worked for CNR and the train company generally turned a blind eye to the unscheduled donations.

When the train was gone, so was the dog. Eddie worried Dusty had gotten too curious with the train. The trains killed a lot of dogs.

Eddie crossed the tracks and stuck his head under his front porch. No dog. He set the coal bucket on the front step and slipped in under the porch; he heard breathing from the dark space underneath. He wiggled through a little hole in the cellar and crawled under the house like a soldier on his elbows and stomach. Spikes pressed through the living room floor, leaving their rusty, pointy ends hanging over the cellar like old torture tools. Eddie took care to avoid getting pierced by one. Dusty was curled up right under the middle of the house. As Eddie pulled himself in close he saw the puppies: a whole litter of half-blind, hungry, scared puppies, pulling at Dusty's teats.

Lying on her side, the dog looked at Eddie. She looked tired but happy. He crawled in beside her and she let the boy snuggle in. He was soon asleep, snoring with the puppies.

5

Eddie started school when he was five, walking down the dirt road to the building, which stood next to Seaview United Baptist Church. It had taken the villagers decades to convince the City they needed and deserved a school, so when they finally got the one-room building in 1883, it became a landmark of pride for Africville.

Early one school morning, Eddie and his brothers and sisters – Uncle Bill and his family had moved out by then – were sitting around the table eating breakfast. Daisy was rushing about, feeding her family before she had to race up the way to Rockingham to clean up a white family's house. She had a lot of jobs to feed a lot of mouths.

Victor was teasing Eddie when a huge bang cracked open the air in front of their house. Everybody froze: they knew what a gunshot sounded like. Clarence was away. Daisy told the kids to stay still while she went to see what had happened, but they followed her anyway.

So everybody got to start the day off the same way: watching a police officer lug the freshly shot body of Dusty off their front lawn. The puppies had scattered and were nowhere to be seen.

Eddie screamed through the window. Victor stared, hard eyes watering. Daisy trembled with rage.

"What are you doing?" she shouted at the cop.

The cop ignored them. Dragged the body into his vehicle and drove off.

It wasn't a big deal. He shot a lot of dogs in Africville. All the cops did: it was just one of the duties an officer was expected to carry out. Everyone in Halifax knew Africville dogs were wild and there was a fear they'd come up over the hill and savage the people. So the cops paid regular trips to Africville and shot loose dogs. Pretty much all the dogs in Africville were loose.

One day, they had the same idea at Curley Vemb's house. He was a big Black Danish man who had fallen in love with an Africville girl and moved all the way across the ocean to be with her. His son Craig was a friend of the Carvery boys. So the cop cocked his gun and pointed it at the head of Curley's dog, who was chained up on the front porch and growling at the intruder. The cop was about to pull the trigger when he heard a tapping on the window.

The cop looked up.

Great big Curley Vemb was standing in his house, pointing his shotgun at the cop's head.

"You pull your trigger, and I'm gonna pull mine," Curley said.

The cop lowered his gun and slowly backed away.

But Curley Vemb was not watching when Dusty got shot. Clarence wasn't at home. So the cop just shot the dog and dumped the body. Daisy did a little emotional triage and got her kids out the door: she still had to go to work and they still had to go to school.

6

The City dump arrived in Africville in the mid-1950s, not long after Eddie was born. It started off in the South End of Halifax, but the South End didn't want it and pushed it up to the North End. The North End didn't want it either, so they pushed it right to the end of the peninsula, over the hill into Africville. And where were they going to push it? Into Bedford Basin? Besides, it fit right into the extensive City services provided in Africville. Up on top of the hill, guarding Africville like a prison wall, was in fact a big, brick prison: Rockhead Prison, built in 1853. Next to that was the Infectious Diseases Hospital, built in 1870. There were also a couple of abattoirs, a bone-mill factory and, for a terribly long time, the City "night-soil deposit."

Night soil is human feces. Back before most people had indoor plumbing, city folks dumped their dung into chamber pots and threw all of that out on the street at night. Workers gathered it up, carted it out of town and dumped it on the hill overlooking Africville. How do you think that smelled? Not like roses.

At first, Africvillians thought the dump was purely awful. Who wouldn't? Who would want their new neighbour to be an open dump? They would have moved it on if they had the economic and political clout, but they didn't. Africville was the end of the line. The dump was dumped there and it wasn't going anywhere. Eventually, some of the poorer and more industrious people of Africville noticed not all of the junk was garbage. People threw out perfectly good windows, doors, clothes, nails and even food. And occasionally booze.

Eddie and his brothers joined the poor and industrious Africvillians at the dump whenever the bread or meat truck arrived. The food was too old to sell to people in the city, but there wasn't anything wrong with it and eating stale bread beat being hungry, so people lined up. They weren't picking it out of the dump: they were taking it out of the truck, just like everybody else in town. Only because it was a day old, and about to be chucked out, it was free. The truck drivers didn't mind – it meant they didn't have to get out of the vehicle and clear the truck out themselves. They just pulled up by the dump and before they even put on the parking brake, people were surrounding them, saying hello and taking turns doling out the food.

One fall day a rumour spread through the party-loving part of Africville that a special delivery had come to the dump. Interested families appointed a head to go down and check it out on a cool day in the late 1950s. Eddie was a young boy and his father was away, so his Carverys weren't interested in the unexpected bonus.

"What is it?" one man shouted up to the white City men who wrestled the big, tightly sealed five-gallon steel containers out of their truck and onto the dump. The men were under orders to break up the containers and pour out the contents, but then all these Black people turned up and started asking what was inside the barrels.

"Alcohol," the City man shouted back with a smile. It wasn't a nice smile. He'd been here many times before and thought of Africvillians as not so different from the rats that scurried under his car when he stopped at the dump at night with a date. It was the sort of thing people did: cruise into Africville late at night, drive to the dump, turn out the lights and hear those rats scurry! Better make sure you don't have any holes in the floor. What a laugh.

"Mix it with your home brew and you'll get a good drunk out of it," he told the Africvillians. There was cheering. The men divvied up the booze.

The City man nodded, smiling.

That night, Africville partied like it was a new millennium. Like Joe Louis was back in town. The Brown Bomber had stayed in Africville once. Everyone listened to his fights on the radio, so it was pretty exciting when he turned up to referee a wrestling match in Halifax. That's how he made his living after he was done with boxing. Joe Louis, the former heavyweight champion of the whole entire world, was in Halifax, staying at a fancy hotel, when he noticed there were no coloured people in it. Or anywhere else, for that matter.

"Where are all the Black people?" the champ asked the hotel manager.

The manager cleared his throat and explained that the hotel didn't usually let coloured people in, but they had made an exception for him.

Louis stared at him with round-twelve eyes. Louis checked out and headed for Africville, staying with Rossie Dixon. Louis knew all about Africville, because he knew all about George Dixon, the first coloured boxing champion, born and raised in Africville. Rossie was some sort of relation, so Joe Louis stayed with him to honour "Little Chocolate."

When Duke Ellington came to Halifax, he stayed in Africville too, hosted by Reggie and Stella Carvery. Duke's wife, Mildred, was a Dixon from Africville, and so was Stella. He wrote that song, "Sophisticated Lady," about Mildred. What a party that would make: Duke leading all the musicians in Africville deep into the night.

Anyway, that was what it was like the Night of the Free Booze. The contents of the containers were mixed up with the diluting home brew, as per orders, and revellers drank deeply, merrily and loudly into the night. Every guitar in Africville was dusted off and the finest – and worst – voices sang increasingly raunchy songs, even though Duke wasn't there to lead them.

Eddie slept uneasily in his room. He and his brothers and sisters occasionally woke to discuss the festivities, to wonder who was yodelling at three in the morning.

Morning brought light to a ghastly situation as screaming wives heralded the dawn. Panic spread through the village as people ran from house to house, finding greater and greater horror. The scale of the catastrophe slowly became apparent. Dozens of men had gone blind overnight. Others crawled the streets in agony and were rushed to hospital. There were bodies dead where they fell at the kitchen table. Bodies in the street, people who didn't make it home. At least three died.

Somebody took a closer look at the sealed containers the City men were disposing of, before they decided to hand them out. They contained alcohol, all right. Wood alcohol.

Paint thinner.

Poison.

When Africvillians worked out what had happened, there was a seething rage. Residents surrounded the City men next time they came out and demanded to know why they had given poison to people.

The City shrugged its shoulders.

"You had no business being on the dump," one supervisor explained. "It's not our fault."

And so it went.

7

Eight-year-old Eddie ran to Kildare's Field. It was summer. Kildare's Field, out by the Skinner house near the end of Africville, was the place to be in the summer if you were a boy in need of play. Eddie and his friends reached Tibby's Pond, which was flush with a high tide smooching the shore. It was a tidal pond, so when the tide was out, the land came up and cut it off. When the tide was in, the whole thing flowed right out into the Basin. It was called Tibby's Pond because Aunt Tibby lived there. She wasn't Eddie's aunt: everyone in Africville was his aunt or uncle, his ma or pa. It was hard sometimes to remember who was your flesh and blood, and who was your community. In the winter, Tibby's Pond froze over and became a skating rink. The Africville Sea Sides used to practise there, when the Coloured Hockey League was going strong. Uncle Pa Carvery, who actually was Eddie's uncle, played defence for the Sea Sides back in 1922.

People used Kildare's Field for sports and picnics, apart from when the Gypsies visited. Then, kids steered clear, as legend had it the Gypsies would snatch children.

His friends hesitated, but Eddie dove right into the salt water, swimming across. Why walk around when you could swim through? Tibby's Pond was where Eddie's mother had taught him to swim. As he swam across, feeling the cool water and the warm air above it, he saw his father out in the Basin in a two-man dory, hauling in some of the giant cod. When Clarence was home, they ate most of what he caught, but he sold some of it to the markets in the city. Other fishing boats were tied up at Tibby's Pond. It was everybody's pond, really.

Eddie got to the other side fine and his friends followed over land. They weren't playing long before things went wrong. "Ew!" his friends shouted, pointing at him. Eddie looked down at his transforming body: a pus blister was forming on his arm. Gooey, oozy sores emerged all over his bronze skin.

"It's nothing," he said, feigning bravado. His voice was shaking, though. He had a bad feeling. He couldn't stop checking his arms, picking at the wounds, which were itching fiercely.

Another one, and another.

He scratched them, feeling sick to his stomach. His friends checked themselves out, but they were both clean. Leeches, he knew about. This was something different.

"You'd better go home," one of his friends told him.

Eddie hesitated. It was a nice day and he was having fun. He didn't want to worry his mother. She didn't get much quiet time, what with her job as a maid up in Rockingham, raising all her own children plus all the white family's children.

The sores got worse.

"I'd better go home," he said to his friends, trying to sound like Mr. Cool. His friends offered to come, but he told them to stay. "I'll be fine."

Eddie ran home, taking care to go around the pond. He noticed now it had a funny colour, a frothy green. The City had hooked a sewer pipe to the Infectious Diseases Hospital that sat fenced off above Africville. They had run that pipe underground and pointed it to empty into Tibby's Pond. So the waste of the city, mixed with the toxic waste of the Infectious Diseases Hospital, poured directly into the swimming hole, mixing with the people, the food and dishes they washed in it, the fish they ate, and even their fine white robes as they praised God and were dunked under water by the minister on baptism day. The City didn't tell anybody in Africville.

"Eddie!" his mother cried when she saw the state of her son. She came from Mi'kmaq people and her grandmothers were healers for generations. She knew how to heal, too. She tried cleaning her son, got him half-way there, but realized she needed help. Granny Pink arrived and reached a startling conclusion: whatever was wrong with Eddie might start being wrong with everybody else in the house, so he had to go get better out of Africville. They packed him off to his Aunt Margaret's house in the countryside, in Sackville. Margaret was actually Eddie's aunt.

Eddie tried not to cry.

"I don't want to go!" he said, holding back the blubbering with quivering lip and watering eyes. "I'm okay!"

He hated leaving Africville, even for just a little bit. Bad things had a way of happening to him when he left Africville.

His mother shook her head. She was not a cold-hearted woman, but she had many children to care for. Eddie needed some distance to heal. She packed him off to Sackville.

"Just look at you," Aunt Margaret muttered, once she'd stripped the boy and stood him in the tub. She used iodine to wash his skin clean; iodine on raw sores hurts like hell. Eddie screamed like a banshee, howled like a hurricane, cried like a monsoon.

Aunt Margaret kept scrubbing the boy in the bathtub, holding his little naked body tight. She did not yield to his sobbing pleas for mercy.

Aunt Margaret was deaf.

"I want to go back to Africville," Eddie wept. "I want to be safe," he whimpered.

Eddie stayed out in Sackville until the sores all went away. That took the whole summer. His cousins, Aunt Margaret's boys, were bigger and bored, so they bullied Eddie, all summer long.

Eddie finally got better.

Eddie went home to Africville.

8

Granny Pink lived at 1893 Barrington Street, just before the pavement ended and Africville began. Her house, the big white one, sat on the main road. Next to her house was a driveway, then three more houses, mostly her relations. Behind her house, the field ran right down to the shore. Near it was a little house in a little field with little apple trees and a white picket fence. That was Eddie's house.

Granny Pink had a real house, with a foundation dug into the ground and everything. A lot of houses didn't have foundations, because you needed a permit for a foundation and nobody could remember the last time Halifax had actually agreed to issue a building permit in Africville. The pavement stopped before Africville, the sewage pipes stopped before Africville and there was no running water in Africville. They had electricity and telephones, though, finally, but it had taken a lot of hard work to pry that from the City.

Granny Pink had a relative living in a house on her property. Uncle Bunny's house was out back of hers. Where did these nicknames come from? Who knows? Anyway, the Big Barn, the pig pen and the chicken coop were behind that, on the water where people emptied out their chamber pots.

Granny Pink's house wasn't just an ordinary house – it was also Africville's post office. She was the first Black postmistress in all of Canada. You just had to put the person's name on the envelope and underneath that write "Africville, Nova Scotia," and it would wind up in their hand.

Granny Pink also had a small store in her post office. Lots of people had stores in Africville. Some were small collections of canned food, soap and essentials; some were barber shops. At the edge of town, Mrs. Brown had a small store. Ida Carvery had a store. So did Aunt Tilly and Uncle Pa Carvery. Entrepreneurial place, Africville.

Across the tracks that divided Africville, the community rose above the Basin with Big Town, the rough area with households like the Flints and the Blacks. Laura Black had a big family and was married to a man from the Bahamas called Blackie Black. That was up the road. Around the turn, following the tracks, the community started again with the sprawling West family. Pa Carvery was down that way too. When Eddie and Victor went around selling the fish their father caught, this was Victor's turf. The Grays lived down here, too. They lost five kids when their house caught fire and the fire department didn't come. People couldn't even buy fire insurance in Africville, it was so well-known that the fire trucks rarely made it out in time.

Towering up on top of the hill were of course Rockhead Prison and the Infectious Diseases Hospital. That's where Africville was born, old Africville, up on the hill, but the first Africville was burnt out and the people driven down to the lower, newer Africville. The land was taken over by the City. The origins of Africville are shapes in the mist, but everyone knows that in 1796, the Maroons arrived and some of them settled in the Black community down on the shore of Bedford Basin.

"I think the man got what he wanted – that Africville land," an elder would one day sigh when it was all over. "It was as simple as that. People were allowed to stay there the same as Black folks anywhere; they could stay until the white man decided, 'Okay, now I want my land back.' And the time came, and he said, 'Okay, nigger, get out!' And the Black folks had to get out."

That's what he said way ahead in 1969. We haven't left the 1950s yet. Eddie's still a little boy.

So Granny Pink ran the post office and knew everyone in Africville and just delivered the letters when she saw people walking by.

"George!" she'd call out. "I've got a letter for you."

And George would come in and get his letter.

Granny Pink knew most of Africville's secrets, too, as a lot of people couldn't read well. They'd sit down with Granny Pink when the post came and she'd read it to them. She'd also help them write the replies and send them out to Winnipeg, or down to the United States, or Montreal, or wherever their family had gone looking to get rich.

Granny Pink's house was the hub of Africville, second only to the church. And maybe the dance hall. The kitchen was big, the living room was fine and there was a dining room as well. Usually, people just had two of those three rooms. Granny Pink had all three, plus a big sun porch on the front of the house. A back porch, too. Up on the second floor was her bedroom and then three more. The post office was in the dining room. She had a nice writing desk and all the materials she needed to run the business.

Granny Pink was also a midwife and Africville's resident psychologist, listening to people's problems and helping them find solutions. For the kids, she always had a piece of pie, or bread, or maybe a bit of candy. The following will come as no surprise: her house was always full, especially once she got the village's first TV. It was nothing for twenty people to pile into her living room to watch the test pattern.

Can you imagine the scene when it actually started broadcasting programs?

Eddie always found a hole to crawl into in the living room when the cowboy shows were on. His favourite was *The Roy Rogers Show*, but he also loved *Howdy Doody*. If it was busy, he'd just snuggle right into Granny Pink's side. She didn't mind.

9

One Saturday morning, Eddie's younger brother Victor wasn't watching Granny Pink's television. He was up in the woods, eyes peeled. He was afraid of strangers. The Gypsies might steal you if you got too close and who knows what the white people would do. He was up there with friends and a big bucket, collecting blueberries for his grandmother to make a pie with. One for him, one for the bucket, one for him, one for the bucket, he ate as many as he collected, popping the juicy berries in his mouth. He was up high, near the edge of Africville, and keeping an eye out for police or other strangers. His mother had warned him against the police.

He tossed some more berries in the bucket and spotted a white man. He was walking off the road, down to the woods. Victor froze. Maybe he was escaped from the prison or the hospital. Maybe he was an off-duty cop, come to shoot dogs or little boys. The man found a rock and sat down in the woods, overlooking the Basin and Africville.

Victor stopped breathing, eyes wide. He slowly backed away, keeping an eye on the man.

The man saw him.

"Hey, nigger boy," the man said, in a friendly sort of way.

Victor turned and bolted, tumbling down the pathway, sprinting by the fort he and his friends had just built, blasting by the apple tree and raspberries.

When he got clear of the woods, he ran straight to his grandmother's house like he was heading for home plate on an inside-the-park home run. Granny Pink was just finishing with helping a man to read his letters when Victor burst in.

"What's wrong?" she asked, pulling his little head to her bosom. She stroked him till he calmed down and started babbling about the white man who had frightened him. The man Granny Pink was helping excused himself and left, letters in hand.

"Let me tell you a story," Granny Pink told Victor. "You're a lucky boy, because you're an Africvillian."

She told him how Africville started out as African Village, long before Canada, almost before Halifax.

"Before the Irish came, before the Germans came, before all the rest of them other cultures came over here, we were here. We were forced to come here, but we were here. Us and the Red Man," she said. "We were paving the roads, building the streets and the buildings. This is where I'm coming from."

She told him about their ancestors, the Maroons.

The Maroons were Jamaicans. They lived in Jamaica at the same time as the British. The British were European people who at the time kept themselves busy by moving onto every bit of land they could find defended by poorly armed people. The British thought it was a good idea that Black people be kidnapped and declared pieces of property, human machines bought and sold and destroyed as needed. When two Black people had a baby, the British thought that baby should become the property of the owners, to be used as a human machine programmed to do various tasks.

The Maroons disagreed. They thought Black people should be free to do what they wanted. The two warrior nations, the British and the Maroons, fought viciously. For years, the Maroons built enclaves in the hills of Jamaica and launched raids on British territory to free British property and turn it back into human beings. Finally, the British told the Maroons to heave off and they'd give them land in Nova Scotia, a piece of the world they had taken 150 years before from people called Mi'kmaq. The Maroons departed Jamaica in shackles on ships bound for a brave new world. On arrival they scattered around the new city of Halifax, built to keep another group of Europeans called the French off the land. Some Maroons set up camp north of the city and got to work building the streets of Halifax. They helped build Citadel Hill, the star-shaped fort that defines the city.

It was a straight land swap, Granny Pink said. The Maroons gave up their Jamaican territory for a chunk of land in Nova Scotia. The land was just outside of Halifax in Preston and also right on the Bedford Basin.

The Maroons joined the militia.

One of the Maroon officers was called Carvery.

"Down there in Jamaica, way back when, when they sent the Maroons up to build Citadel Hill, the Jamaican government paid Canada for a property for their Maroons to live on. That land was Africville," Granny Pink told Victor.

Victor sat up, looking into her warm eyes.

"My grandfather came to Nova Scotia in shackles with the Maroons," she said. "This was Crown land because of the work we done after we came here. For services we had done for the country. They deeded us this Crown land. We were the ones that were the farmers. We were the ones that were the carpenters. We were the ones that were the masons. We were the ones that were the labourers. We were the ones that were the housemaids. We had a value, a worth. We were needed. That's why we were deeded this place right here," she told him, looking out over Africville.

After a few years, most of the Maroons un-marooned themselves from the discrimination and ill will of Nova Scarcity and packed up once more, this time heading back to Africa, to Sierra Leone.

But not everybody left. Some remained. One of them, history whispers, was called Carvery.

Victor smiled. His eyes were heavy. He felt warm and safe. He felt like having a nap. Granny Pink had that effect on him.

10

The five-ton truck backed up to the dump and poured out a gleaming load of knife-sharp tin-can tops. Thousands of shining disks tumbled out onto the garbage, spilling down the sides. Too small for the peanut butter cans they were designed for, they were being thrown out.

Eddie and his friends couldn't believe their luck. The boys stood, amazed, astounded the truck was just going to leave the tops right there.

The back of the dump truck reversed, landing on the chassis with a thump. The driver pulled away, barely glancing at the half a dozen boys watching in awe.

"War!" one shouted and they raced to gather the weaponry.

Eddie filled a cardboard box with the disks of death, cutting himself only a couple of times. He sucked the blood off his hand. The boys split into two warring factions and he sprinted down the mountain of trash seeking cover before his enemies attacked.

"Zooonk!" screamed the makeshift ninja star as it flew past his bushy hair. Eddie hollered and dove into the bushes, hands searching the undergrowth.

The boys experimented with the ninja stars, finding the best angle to fling them at to ensure maximum devastation. A few early casualties took death stars to the ribs and scrambled for cover.

Eddie dug deeper under the bush.

His hand found something solid.

It was there.

He was safe.

He emerged from the bushes holding his indestructible trash can top in front of him like a shield. The next flying can top zonked on in, crashed into the trash can lid like a cymbal on a drum and fell harmlessly to the ground.

He laughed.

"War!" he shouted, storming an enemy platoon of boys. It took him a moment to perfect the technique of protecting himself with the shield while attacking with the lids, but he quickly got the hang of it and advanced.

One lucky shot angled down from above, bypassing his shield and cutting into his foot. Eddie screamed, hopping around in agony. He fell over, clutching his toes.

He grew still.

The war paused.

The tin-can soldiers hesitated, hoping Eddie was not fatally wounded.

"Eddie? You okay?" asked the boy who had thrown the lucky shot.

No reply.

The boy walked slowly to Eddie, who was clutching his bleeding foot.

And his flying lids.

The boy got within ten feet before Eddie fired the razor-sharp weapon at him.

"Ah! Cheater!" the boy shouted as the lid caught him in the belly, bouncing off his shirt. The boy turned and ran for his shield and weapon cache, Eddie following in sprinting battle mode.

The boy raced to the wheat cars stopped on the train tracks, leaping on top and darting across, jumping from car to car. Eddie followed and behind him, the other warriors charged as one.

"Where are you?" Eddie challenged, standing atop a big, black tank car. "Come out, coward!"

The other boy warriors waited together on the car behind.

This was a two-man duel now.

Eddie suddenly looked down. The door on top of the tank car was partially ajar. He unscrewed it and leapt inside.

The tank was huge in the pitch black. Eddie moved cautiously in the dark, feeling his way along, the edge of his shield scraping against the wall. He was worried the other boy's eyes had better adjusted to the lack of light and he would use his advantage to counterattack.

Eddie's shield banged into the side of the empty car, scaring him half to death.

He composed himself and continued the search. The walls wobbled. Eddie staggered. His eyes were picking up the light coming in through the roof opening, showing him pockets of emptiness. He listened sharply. He could hear the boys above, but nothing inside.

What was that?

He leapt sideways to avoid an attack but lost his balance and fell to the floor. He held his shield up to protect himself against the final assault.

Nothing came.

Eddie stood woozily to his feet, the toxic fumes of the tank unsettling his mind.

"He's down there!" shouted an ally from above.

Eddie steadied himself, but it was hard, what with his head spinning like a top. He tossed his weapons and shield up on the sunny roof and stuck his hands through the opening. The other boys, eager to see the fight continue, hauled him out and pointed him at his fleeing foe.

The fresh air cleared his head. "War!" he shouted, rattling his shield and lids menacingly, staggering after his vanishing enemy.

11

Eddie was at home when the news came. It was summer, about 1953. A neighbour whispered it to his mother.

"Oh my God," Daisy moaned, swooning against the wall. She dropped everything and ran out of the house.

Eddie had never seen his mother run and it scared him. He and his older brother Dickie followed as fast as their short legs could carry them.

He could hear his mother wailing as he got around the turn by the dump. A man grabbed him hard and stopped him on the train tracks as Dickie ran on. "You can't see that," the man said, holding the pushing and kicking boy tightly. But Eddie could see it.

It was his older brother, Raymond. Raymond was thirteen and working the dump. Who wasn't? It was money and money was needed.

The problem was that Raymond was lying on the dirty road below, broken in two.

Word swept through Africville like fire. Mothers held their children close, crying. Raymond's friend Harold stood nearby, horror-struck. He kept repeating his story to anyone who would listen. Eddie listened.

The two friends had jumped on an arriving dump truck to get first dibs on the newspapers on board. They were good for starting fires. The dump truck driver spotted the boys and took off with a jolt. The boys tried to jump down but the driver spun off the dump, moving too fast for them to escape. Raymond spilled back and grabbed the first thing he could to hang onto the speeding truck. It was a blistering hot muffler that scorched his hands. He fell. The five-ton truck ran him over and then just drove on into Halifax. Harold fell too, but rolled safely away.

"He knew we were on the truck, 'cause he told us he ain't gonna let us off. He said, 'You ain't gonna get away' and sped off," said Harold, who everyone called Puppy.

The official story? The boys had no business being on the truck, the driver hadn't seen them anyway, and that was the end of that.

Eddie watched as Africville gathered to bury his big brother.

12

Eddie had two fathers: the mostly decent man who worked hard to provide for his family before Raymond died and the alcoholic, violent womanizer who replaced him. Clarence was ravaged by guilt. He had encouraged his son to work the dump to help the family scrape by, so he felt responsible for his death. The guilt eroded his goodness.

Eddie's father would head into the city for a day of drinking and gambling and if things went badly, he'd bring the badness home. It was terrible if you happened to be standing in his way – he'd beat you half to death. If you'd actually done something wrong, it was like being attacked by Joe Louis in his prime.

When Daisy saw Clarence coming home in a ferocious anger, she'd warn the kids.

"Your father's drinking, get outta sight," she said in strained tones, shooing her children away.

They'd run and jump into trunks, crawl into the walls, pull themselves into the ceiling, under the steps, into antique boxes or dive under the house in the cellar. The bedrooms had bay windows, so the kids would jimmy the boards up and hide in the bones of the house. Eddie's older brother Dickie was the best. He could hide so well he'd never be found.

Their father became a mean man and the kids didn't want to see him, even if he wasn't plotting violence. When Eddie and his brothers and sisters got away, Daisy didn't. There was no wall for her to crawl into – she had to stand up and get knocked down. After, the old man would crash on the sofa and sleep it off. The kids would crawl out of the walls and ceilings, quietly resuming life, tending to Daisy's latest wounds.

One time, Eddie and Victor were up in the bedroom. Eddie was playing with fire. Victor was snoozing, covered in blankets, when Eddie accidentally set the place alight with a pack of matches. He saw the fire, saw the furious punishment his father would mete out, and decided to take his chances with the flames. He climbed under the bed, pried open the box springs and hauled himself inside.

The house caught on fire, but people were home and saw the flames licking through the living room ceiling and so everybody cleared out. The Carvery luck was high that day, as the fire department made it out and got the blaze under control. Daisy was frantic, though, because Eddie was nowhere to be found.

A fireman stomped through the bedroom in his heavy boots, clearing out the burnt-out items. He picked up the bed and watched in amazement as a boy dropped out of it.

Eddie stared at the fireman in terror.

The fireman stared back in amazement.

The room was smoke-damaged, but the house was saved. Eddie's father got home and went into a rage. Eddie took the brunt of it.

13

Clarence lived less and less at home, staying with women, staying out drinking in town or around the turn, only coming home when he felt the need to put his world in order. He'd lose everything and come home fighting mad.

It was the children's job to cut wood and make sure there was enough to keep the house warm. And to keep the water supply filled. If someone slipped up, or they used more than normal, he'd flip out.

"How come you didn't do that?" their father would ask, pointing to the empty kindling basket.

Eddie and his siblings knew there was no answer to this. Out would come the belt, or a stick, or whatever was to hand, and justice would be served one welt at a time.

Most dads in Africville weren't like that. There was a pride in providing for your family, in raising your kids. Uncle Lee, Uncle Bunny, Uncle Bully, Uncle Bill – they were good dads. Eddie's father was a wild card prone to decking people.

After the fire, Victor wasn't home a lot. He'd caught tuberculosis and spent most of his time in hospitals. Lots of people in Halifax had TB in the 1950s and the hospitals would care for them as best they could, keeping them warm with comfortable blankets. Then, they threw the TB blankets in the dump, so lots of Africville people got sick with the disease. Victor spent a lot of his childhood in hospitals.

14

In 1956, Eddie, then a growing boy of ten, was up in the woods when he saw a friend speed past.

"Fire!" the friend shouted breathlessly, not stopping his sprint. "The dump is on fire!"

Eddie dropped what he was doing and ran home as fast as he could. He barrelled in past a dazed Uncle Sonny and up to the children's room. Evelyn walked in and sighed as her dirty brother dug frantically in the closet.

"Where are you going?" she asked, but Eddie kept on digging. He found his old, thick coat, pants, shoes and a pair of gloves he had found in the dump and pulled it all on. He shot down the stairs like a clumpy bullet.

"Are you going to the dump? Just be careful!" Evelyn called as her brother galloped down the street.

Eddie arrived puffing, but relieved to see the fire hadn't really started yet. He nodded to the other scavengers. The bulldozer slowly piled the immense waste heap even higher so a dump truck could fit in one more load from Camp Hill Hospital. It tipped its blood-soaked rags, dirty sheets and needles into the open dump. Eddie wrinkled his nose.

He'd once found a finger in the hospital trash. There were rumours people had found limbs and little dead babies, all trash from the hospitals of Halifax.

The City was busy tearing down old Halifax along Market, Grafton and Hollis Streets and bringing the wreckage here.

Gold mine!

The ad-hoc recycling businesses of Africville were turning trash into a steady stream of income. People were pulling food, clothes, furniture and sellable items out of the dump and using them themselves, or selling stuff in the city. The dump was a killer, but it was also a pillar of the Africville economy.

Today, the dump was massive: three wobbling, stinking stories high, stretching half a football field long and the same width across. The yellow trucks pulled up and dumped their junk, then sped off. One guy did an amazing thing. His dumper didn't work, so he drove up to the top of the heap and angled his truck so the front wheels were hanging over the edge. Then he gunned it and the truck leapt down the hill, scattering trash behind it. It was pretty slick driving. People would stop to watch when they saw the truck coming. Bulldozers patrolled the dump, pushing rubbish around. When the bulldozers were done, Eddie and the others walked onto the dump, placing markers where they spotted aluminum, copper or any other valuable metal. Eddie's keen eye spotted several buried gems under rubber in the busted skeletons of the homes and he planted a stick to mark the spot. Sometimes, the good metal was inside of wood or rubber and you had to time it so you got it when the wood was burnt off, but not the metal.

Tricky work.

Sometimes the cops showed up and made it even trickier. Eddie couldn't work out why they periodically turned up and chased everyone off the dump like they were going to arrest them for salvaging items to avoid going hungry, but they did it with gusto.

They did it because the City said you needed a permit to work the dump.

Who gets a permit to salvage trash?

When the cops turned up, everyone ran and hid till they left. Once, Eddie hid in a cardboard box, which a bulldozer proceeded to bulldoze right over the edge of the dump. Eddie scrambled out seconds before it plummeted over.

Eddie's partner on the dump in those days was his cousin Mannie. They hadn't always been friends – in fact, they started out as enemies. Every time the two met, they'd duke it out. Then they'd go to their homes and get beaten again for fighting. Eddie could never work that one out.

Eventually, though, the two boys saw that life would go better if they stopped pounding each other every chance they got. So they teamed up and hit the dump. The two boys were the hardest workers there. They'd even go right for the car engines, prying and hauling the big motors out of abandoned trucks and cars. It was a two-boy job, so Mannie and Eddie learned to work together.

Most days, they'd get to the dump at about six o'clock in the morning so they could be there when Swift or Canadian Packers Meat Company brought their loads out. Another favourite was the Oland's Beer truck. Not only could they get the bottles to collect, but sometimes there was actual beer on board. Eddie'd grab that and crack open a cold one. He was doing a man's job, so he figured he deserved a man's drink.

Apart from the booze and the food, the dump gave Eddie a job. He could earn money and bring it to Daisy. The boy felt like a man when he handed her his earnings. She'd smile, hug him and put it somewhere safe.

After a morning at the dump, Eddie'd clean up and head to school for the day. After school it was time for chores, then back to the dump for an evening shift, until it got dark.

Once, Eddie and his friends found a big pile of clothes, papers, posters and flags, all with the same red background, white circle and crooked cross. They had no idea what it meant, but they knew sharp threads when they saw them. Everybody grabbed some gear and strutted around the dump in the faux-military duds. Eddie strutted all the way home before his mother met him at the door. Her eyes just about popped out of her head as she told her son to take that Nazi stuff back to the dump where he'd found it.

Eddie worked the dump for years, until he was big enough to land a job on a fishing boat sailing out of the South End. For the rest of his life, if he wasn't in Africville, he was probably at sea. Anything else usually led him into trouble.

"Clear out!" a man shouted and everybody scrambled off the mountain. City workers set the fire and soon the heat drove back all but the bravest. Eddie tightened his gloves. They were way too big for his hands. They'd had fallen off once. That had hurt like hell.

The incinerating fire swept through the dump, noisy and hot like a dragon with a chest infection. Eddie took a deep breath, memorized the locations of the markers, and ran into the inferno.

"It's time to dance in the fire!" he shouted and the scavengers raced into the blaze. The City workers shook their heads as the fire scavengers pulled out the copper first. Eddie waited for the fire to sear off the rubber and grabbed the red-hot chunk of ready-to-sell metal. He spotted some lead already melting in the heat but let it go. Unlike other metals, lead just puddled and resolidified after the fire. You could get it then without risking your life. You still had to grab it fast, though, or someone else would beat you to it.

Eddie watched the development of the fire closely as it burned around him. The dump was stuffed with timber from the old city houses and blazing ferociously. Flames would leap out of the ground and incinerate an area in seconds, or burn deep under the surface and cause the top junk to collapse into a fiery pit. One mistake could lead to a very painful death.

The tar roofing was smoking now. Dark black pillars billowed out of the burning dump. Eddie breathed in a lungful of smoldering tar-smoke and fell to his knees gagging, coughing and spitting into his sleeve. He tried to clear his mind so he wouldn't do something stupid, like walk into the hospital waste and get stabbed by a needle. He wasn't scared – you couldn't be scared, not here, not now.

The arm of his coat caught fire. He shook his head and ran to a safer part of the dump he had marked for copper, batting the flames off his arm. Part of the dump gave way under his feet, but he managed to sidestep the blue-hot flames and dance along to more solid ground. He grabbed handfuls of metal and added it to his pile. This dump work was only for the hungriest Africvillians, those who had to hustle hard to survive. Those who didn't have a stable father watching out for them. Those like Eddie.

He could see others in the black haze, using serious tools like hooks and chains to haul out whole beams of red-hot steel. The dump was molten lava now, the boiling belly of an erupting volcano, and Eddie grabbed one more handful before leaping off. The other exhausted, filthy fire scavengers had already gotten clear and were counting their takings. Eddie looked over his. He'd take it to the junk store on Lady Hammond Road later. He figured it was worth eighty dollars.

He smiled, pleased with the day's takings, gathered his goods and went home to wash up for bed.

15

Grinning, Eddie opened the front door of the little white school building called Mulgrave Park Annex. It was 1954 and grade three was going to be a good year. His grades had been good in Africville's school up to grade two. It was such a nice little school, right next to the church – nice enough that Portia White once taught there before she became a world-famous singer. She sang in the church, too. The City bulldozed the school when Eddie was eight.

Make way! Progress coming through! Segregation was the last thing any modern city wanted and so it was time for some integration. Funnily enough, integration always seemed to go one way, with Black people having to integrate into the white people's world.

So the little Africville school was reduced to a heap of broken bones and the students integrated into the city schools.

No problem. How different could it be?

Eddie was fearless.

The bright boy's happy progress down the white-walled school was stopped by two white women.

One was old and ill-tempered. She had an ugly wart on her chin and peered at Eddie through chunky glasses. She packed 190 angry pounds around her five-foot-tall frame. In truth, she went around as much as she went up and down. She looked like she was in agony and wanted to share the pain.

Eddie thought of Witch Hazel, arch nemesis of Bugs Bunny.

What's up, Teach?

The other lady was young and pretty. She smiled warmly at Eddie and when she spoke, she revealed a cute Newfoundland accent.

Eddie fell in love with her on the spot.

The two white women looked at the little Black boy.

The little Black boy looked at them.

He smiled.

The younger woman smiled back.

The old hag didn't.

"Excuse me, sir," the old crow said with exaggerated politeness. "My name is Mrs. Beck and this is Miss MacGillvray. Which classroom would you like to go in?"

Her eyes were narrow slits. Her mouth was a mean, thin line.

Behind her rumpled bottom was her classroom. Behind the petite derrière of Miss MacGillvray was her classroom.

Eddie took 0.5 seconds to decide.

"I'll go with her classroom," he said, pointing to the pretty young woman.

"You just made the biggest mistake of your life," the old hag cackled.

"What do you mean?" asked Eddie, suddenly afraid.

"Well, in the first place, she's the substitute. I'm the teacher."

The hag smiled with wicked satisfaction.

Eddie was unfazed.

"That's all right, but Mom told me I'm smart and I'm going to grade into grade four and then I won't have you for my teacher," he answered, smartly, smiling.

The young teacher stifled a giggle.

The old hag snarled down at the little boy.

"Yeah, I'm going to get you next year," she vowed.

The old woman and the young boy stared at each other.

"Come on then, Eddie," Miss MacGillvray finally said, taking Eddie by the hand. She led him into her classroom. He watched Mrs. Beck over his shoulder as she stood brooding.

When Miss MacGillvray opened the classroom's door, Eddie's jaw hit the floor. He couldn't believe what he was seeing. He rubbed his eyes in amazement. They were still there. It was like a zoo full of unicorns.

It was rows and rows and rows of white children.

Not a Black face in sight.

"Class, this is Eddie Carvery," the teacher said.

The well-mannered class said, "Hello."

Eddie stared.

Eddie thought, he didn't fit in in Africville because his brown skin was too light – his mother's mother was Mi'kmaq and her father was Scottish. His dad's side was Black.

Eddie was bronze.

Maybe he'd fit in with these pale children.

His mind boggled.

The kids tittered.

It was like the world had reversed polarity and all the Black faces had turned white. He had never dreamed there were that many white people in the whole world, let alone in one classroom.

"Would you like to have a seat, Eddie?" Miss MacGillvray asked.

He took a breath and navigated the sea of white and sat in an empty desk.

He tried not to stare at the unicorns.

16

Eddie had a very good year with Miss MacGillvray and he easily graduated, just like his mother had told him he would. The next year he proudly took a seat in Miss Miller's grade four class. It wasn't just any old desk: it was a big, left-handed desk, so lefty Eddie could write comfortably.

On the first day of the new year, as Miss Miller was welcoming her new students, the classroom door banged open and the old hag from grade three walked in.

"Well, hello, Mrs. Beck," said a surprised Miss Miller.

The old hag said nothing, scowling as she marched directly to Eddie's desk. The class watched in slack-jawed and wide-eyed fear as she closed in on the nine-year-old boy, grabbed him by the arm and pulled him out of the classroom.

"What are you doing? What are you doing?" he shrieked in protest.

"You're coming back in grade three," she rumbled like an angry crocodile.

"No, no! I graded!" Eddie shouted. "I passed! I'm not coming back!"

"You're coming back," she said, dragging Eddie to the door.

She hauled Eddie down the hall, shoved open her grade three door and manhandled the boy to a tiny, right-handed desk at the front of the class, right next to her. The growing boy barely fit in it. Mrs. Beck squished him into it.

The class of eight-year-olds watched in dumb terror.

Mrs. Beck smoothed her dress and started the lesson.

Eddie soon accepted this setback. What's a year when you're young? He worked hard, studied long into the night and notched up a string of good grades.

Mrs. Beck tore his papers up in his face.

"You'll be back next year," she said, scattering the pieces of his exams. "I don't care how much you make, how many hundreds you get, you are not leaving."

Six years later, fifteen-year-old Eddie Carvery slunk into Mrs. Beck's grade five class. His string of failed grades ended when Mrs. Beck moved to grade four and took Eddie with her. When she got to grade five, so did he. He'd been stuck there with her since. His classmates kept getting smaller. So did his desks. Sometimes he did the work, more often he didn't. Why bother?

One year, two pretty, blond Danish exchange students joined the class. The girls couldn't speak English, but soon became the teacher's pets, charming the charmless Mrs. Beck. She graded them, even though they could barely speak English.

Eddie's youngest brother Irvine started school in 1956, one year after the Black kids were integrated into the white schools. Teachers were at a loss all over the city. At Mulgrave Park, they'd never taught Black kids before. They'd barely seen Black people. How they talked, how they moved, how they behaved – it was like they were aliens from another planet. A planet the teachers had heard a lot of things about, most of them not good.

While Eddie got body-checked out of the education system, Irvine slipped through the school system like Pa Carvery cutting up the ice for the Africville Sea Sides hockey team. He skipped grade four and caught up to his older brother in grade five. Mrs. Beck loved Irvine. Eddie loved Irvine. Everyone loved Irvine. Eddie was two brothers older than Irvine, but there they were, together again, in the classroom of Mrs. Beck. Eddie sat in his usual seat at the front of the classroom while Irvine quietly worked his way to the head of the class. Eddie skipped school a lot.

"I'm going to leave," he told Irvine. "I'm going to get a job."

Irvine could see Eddie wasn't great at school, but he also saw teachers didn't understand his older brother and weren't prepared to listen to him. Irvine watched as eighty percent of the Africville students were bundled off to the bungalow auxiliary class for "slow" learners. Irvine knew eighty percent of his friends weren't slow learners. He knew Mrs. Beck was Eddie's nemesis, a brick wall that busted his head.

"That's the way it is sometimes," Irvine mused. He was a good, unassuming boy. He liked learning, he liked school. He was Black and he knew Mrs. Beck was racist, but he knew how to play her. Eddie, on the other hand, was Black and couldn't understand why that mattered. Mrs. Beck made it her duty to teach him why it mattered. Irvine slipped by on her periphery.

As grade five got underway again, Eddie trundled to his seat at the front, a man among children. He stuffed himself into the right-handed desk built for a ten-year-old boy, glaring at the wicked witch as she smiled vindictively and started the whole torment over again.

As she did every year, she started by calling Eddie up to the front of the class.

He tugged himself out of the tiny desk and slouched to the blackboard, standing beside his perpetual teacher with slumped shoulders, eyes on the floor as his cheeks burned in shame.

"This is what you must never be like," Mrs. Beck told the children, indicating the ramshackle wreckage of a failed pupil. She dramatically held up her hand and counted Eddie's failings on her fingers. "He's a liar, he stinks, his hair is never clean, his teeth are rotted and falling out, his skin is greasy and dirty and his clothes are grotesque rags."

The children gasped in horror as they swallowed the old witch's toxic brew. They could not look away from Eddie and his beastly failure.

Eddie didn't stink, he kept clean and his teeth were fine. But still.

"Don't go near him. He's contagious. You don't want his disease," the teacher concluded, dismissing him for another year.

Eddie slouched back to his seat and jammed himself in, head down. His new classmates recoiled in disgust. He recoiled too, disgusted by himself. He thought he was no good. He thought he was supposed to mess up. He thought that all the things she said, she was telling the truth.

That was how every class started.

At recess, he didn't bother getting out of his desk. He had been in detention for six years. He never got to talk to his classmates, never got a chance to set the record straight. One year, lonely, isolated Eddie managed to befriend a Black girl, one of the rare non-white faces in the school. The girl got expelled for her poor choice in friends.

So he just sat there while Mrs. Beck marked papers and kids played outside. After school, she dragged him down to the principal's office.

"Come on," she said. Eddie wasn't sure of this principal's name. There had been so many. They were all the same.

Mrs. Beck told the principal what Eddie had done wrong that day, but he didn't bother to listen. It didn't make a difference. There was nothing to learn here.

The principal frowned, shook her head at this monstrous grade five student who was almost as big as her.

Eddie stuck out his hands unprompted. The principal brought out the stick belatedly. The middle-aged woman put all of her strength into pounding the boy's hands, all the while gently telling him it was for his own good, that sometimes people needed harsh correction to show them the error of their ways.

At least this one didn't try to make him cry. Mrs. Beck drove the previous principal to beat Eddie until he cried.

Eddie dreamed of the day he would turn sixteen and could drop out.

17

Dinky Jones had it made. He had a real dad who had a cool job: he was a musician and he blew the trumpet so good it made the earth dance. He was away in Montreal all the time for work, playing in a big band, and when he came home to Africville, everyone stayed up late hearing his stories. He always had something for his kids, too, some new toy nobody had ever dreamed of before. Dinky was lucky and generous. Every time he got a new toy, he handed an old one to his best friend Eddie Cavery. Dinky, Eddie and another friend had a secret society that Irvine and his friends were barred from.

"You can't come near here," Eddie'd warn his younger brother as he approached the clubhouse. "If you get caught, you'll catch a beating!"

Irvine was too slick to get caught, but he never figured out what they were up to, either. He couldn't wait to get old enough to join the society. No one knew what they did, but everyone wanted to do it.

One lazy summer day before he quit school, Eddie caught the eye of Dinky's sister Kay. He'd been in love with her as long as he could remember, but it was a secret affair up until then. So secret not even Kay knew about it. He let her in on his heart's intentions and she found matching beats in her own. They pitched a little tent back in the field near the water and they got married in it. They weren't churched – nor did they tell anyone else about it – but they knew they were bound together forever.

Eddie's heart glittered like the Bedford Basin bathed in morning sun. He wrote poetry for Kay and whispered it to her as they lay in the grass, watching clouds and listening to the waves kissing the shore.

They kissed each other.

Life was good.

Then Dinky's dad blew the only sour note of his life. He came home from Montreal grinning and soon the news was all over Africville. He'd found a new home and was moving his family to Montreal. Everyone was excited – except for Eddie and Kay. The news devastated the couple and they made sacred plans to wait for each other always. Fighting back tears, they walked down to their tent to say their last goodbye.

Then, they were gone, Eddie's best friend and girlfriend in one swoop.

Eddie stayed in the tent by the water, watching the rising tide eat the shore as the clouds consumed the sky.

18

Eddie's puppy love tent was comfortable. Why wouldn't he stay there? By then, the Carverys were living in a barn. When Eddie was twelve, his father took him and the rest of the family out of the house that he and his siblings were born in and put them in Eddie's uncle's pig pen. Well, not exactly a pig pen: a big barn, built for animals but adapted for humans. The rent in Eddie's birth house was too steep, and work too scarce, for Eddie's father to pay for it. So he moved his family into the converted barn built on the back of the shore. Granted, it was bigger than most houses, but it was built to house pigs and chickens, not people, so it was ferociously cold. It was also right on the scenic shoreline where locals brought their sewage deposits to tip into the Basin.

Open your nose wide: it didn't smell like roses.

Eddie's father converted the barn into a house and put his family in it. Then, he left.

Winter had no trouble getting in and turning Eddie's bone marrow to ice. The harbour wind blasted in from the Atlantic, swirled around the harbour, then smacked right through the walls. It blew the sewage stench in with it for good measure.

It wasn't a nice part of Africville.

Still, it was lively. Victor and Irvine were popular and always had friends over and so Eddie's broken heart mostly went unnoticed. Dickie, their oldest surviving brother, still lived at home, working at Dominion Coal Company for a bit and then the seal abattoir. Their older sister Evelyn was home in the barn, too, with all of her kids. She had five by then, with more on the way. That house was a loud place and Eddie didn't even have the solace of a cellar to crawl into to cuddle with his dog.

When he needed a break in the summer, he'd head for the fields and forests and waters around Africville. When he needed a break in the winter, he headed to Granny Pink's to watch the workings of the post office and grab a piece of pie.

When you lived in Africville, you lived in all of Africville, so the fact that your house was a barn in fancy clothing didn't matter all that much.

Except in the winter.

When it was very, very cold.

19

While Eddie suffered through a never-ending grade five, Victor wound up in prison.

It started with a walk in 1960. Victor, then twelve years old, went for a stroll with Granny Pink. She told him a terrible story as they climbed high up the hill of Africville, heading for a spot where they could look straight down on her big white house, on the whole colourful town, on the shimmering blue Basin beyond.

Rockhead Prison and the Infectious Diseases Hospital were at their backs, the rusty old chain-link fences winding through the trees. The stout woman and the bony boy walked side by side as they mounted the steep path.

Granny Pink told her grandson a story from way back in time, back when Africville was a baby, back in the early 1800s. Back then, Africville went up and over Needham Hill and out along the shoreline to Fairview.

"Africville was bigger than Halifax, then," she said in her storyteller voice. "Years later, there were two gentlemen. Their task was to build a railroad from here to Vancouver. They had no money, so they went to the British."

Granny Pink puffed out her belly, stuck out her chin and boomed out in an English accent, making Victor laugh.

"The British said, 'Go to the Black country and sell flesh, human flesh.'"

Victor's laughter died.

Victor remembers Granny Pink telling him how they built that railroad, stealing Black people out of Africville and selling them as slaves to the States.

Granny Pink remembers another story. One day, long ago, two Africville girls were raped by soldiers up on Citadel Hill. People in Africville were mad. There was talk of revenge.

Granny Pink told him how the white boss man of the City went for a walk one day, looked over toward thriving Africville, with its farmlands, fisheries and industry, and announced, "We have a problem. There are more of them than there are of us," Granny Pink quoted, using that English accent and rubbing her belly like a hungry hyena.

"He was to drive them far away from the city," she told wide-eyed Victor. "Bounties were out – any Black person outside of the Black community was in danger. They risked being shot."

Victor and Granny Pink walked farther up the hill in Africville, nodding to neighbours, before stopping in a small field by a tree that bore no fruit. She told him the people who died in the struggle with the City, they were buried here. That's why the tree never bloomed.

Victor danced his feet off the ground to try to avoid standing on his murdered ancestors.

"This is where they buried them," Granny Pink repeated, looking sadly out over the Basin on the quiet, sunny day.

This is the kind of history not written in any books, but seared in the souls of those who tell and retell the terrible tales.

Trembling with rage and shame, Victor dropped Granny Pink's hand and ran down the hill. He ran so fast he almost fell over. He ran straight to an abandoned brick building with a name written on the side, the name of one of the men who had enslaved Africvillians. The big brick building stood on the tracks just beyond Africville and Victor threw stones at the windows, determined to break them all.

He got inside, walked around the derelict building, imagining slaves passing through this hell on their way to an American plantation. He threw more rocks, breaking windows from the inside.

Victor was still throwing stones when the police arrived. Big, burly white cops from Halifax. They scooped up the boy and tossed him in the van. The doors didn't open again until the van was safely in the courtyard of Rockhead Prison, the meanest adult jail in Nova Scotia.

20

Victor was a hard boy and he tried to be tough in prison, but there are some seriously tough men in prison. Victor realized this when the van stopped in the yard of Rockhead Prison and dumped him out. Nobody knew why he was there. Victor didn't know. He thought he'd been forgotten by the world.

"Ain't I supposed to go to court or something for breaking those windows?" he asked the guard.

"No, you're going here. See that gatehouse over there? Line up with the rest of the men," the guard said.

He lined up. He was little, but he was given the same jobs as the men. He was to shovel coal off a truck. He had to wrestle with a shovel that was bigger than he was to beat the clock.

"If you're late, you'll go to number eight," the guards taunted him.

He didn't know what number eight was. He hoped to keep it that way and so shovelled hard.

Some of the prisoners looked out for the child inexplicably thrown in the lion's den. Others tried to chew off a piece of his young flesh.

Rockhead Prison was also a farm. It needed planters in the spring and harvesters in the winter. If it was short on bodies, the cops would round up any stray Black men and pack them off to prison.

Maybe the cops who picked up Victor mistook the boy for a man.

After a while in prison, Victor was ordered to do quarter duty. Not too bad, eh? Actually, awful. Quarter duty was prison code for scraping human feces off the walls of the room where the prisoners dumped their personal sewage.

Victor had dreamed of being a bridge-building engineer, a plane-flying pilot and a boat-sailing captain. Dung-scraper was not an occupation he had dreamt about. Maybe it could still happen, he thought, as he threw chemicals at the dirty walls. The stench was worse than Africville's dump and seal abattoir bottled together on the hottest summer day. He was stuck right in the dung hole, and it stank like he was inside the anus of a monster with bad hygiene.

Still, it was safer than being out in the yard. Victor often asked to be locked up, just to be safe from the crazy men in the prison. The guards didn't care so they let him stay in his cell while the men exercised. Victor sat trembling on his bed, puzzling over how he'd wound up in prison.

They made him clean dung off the walls again. They ordered him to do it again after that. He swallowed back puke with every breath in the dark, fecal hole. A man threw slop in while he was down there, splashing his threadbare clothes. The toxic chemicals he used to burn the human excrement off the walls burned the skin off his eyeballs, too, but he dared not rub his eyes, lest something worse get in.

Victor decided that whatever number eight was, whatever happened to bad prisoners, it could be no worse than working in the toilet of humanity.

He was dispatched to the dung hole again.

"I won't do it," he said firmly, arms crossed defiantly.

"Are you refusing duty?" the guard asked, eyes raised. There was no anger in his voice. Just surprise, as though his shovel had told him it was beat and would be taking the day off.

"Yes," the boy answered, swallowing.

The guard stared hard at him. The guard lifted his truncheon and knocked Victor on the head. The boy crashed to the ground unconscious. The guards grabbed him under the armpits and threw him into the root cellar.

21

Victor awoke in darkness and felt the planks under him shifting. His head ached, he was dazed, he hadn't eaten for days. Root cellar. He remembered he was in the prison root cellar. He put his hand on the floor to see if it was swirling, or if it was just his head.

He ran his hand over the ground.

The ground ran over his hand.

Victor screamed and ran, but walls sent him flying back in every direction. The rats were everywhere.

He stood in the corner shaking, trying to lift his feet off the ground fast enough so he wasn't touching it long enough for the rats to touch him. It was a strange-looking dance in the dark.

Victor screamed until his voice was gone. He was tired, then he was exhausted, then he entered a new zone of consciousness that felt like a living death. He couldn't stop jumping off the ground for fear of the rats, but his legs didn't have the juice to keep lifting him. His eyes never picked up light in the darkness.

Eventually, the guards opened the roof, rushed in and threw a hood over his head while he stood dazed in the daylight. They dragged Victor blindly along the prison, doors clinking open and shut as they progressed out of the lower circles of hell. The hood was torn off his head.

He blinked in the brightness. He wobbled on unsteady legs, adjusting to the unmoving ground. He was in the warden's office.

The warden looked over some papers on his desk.

The guards stood beside the boy.

Victor started to think he must've actually died and was now a ghost, which would explain why no one could see him. This must be St. Peter's opposite number at the gates of hell.

The warden spoke.

"Are you going to be refusing orders again, or are you going to be doing your duties?" the warden asked, staring at the boy.

Victor shook his aching head.

"No! No, I'm not going to do that. I don't care what you do – you can kill me if you want. All I want to do is go home," he said, fighting off tears.

He failed, bursting out in a hot flood of tears.

The root cellar was awful, all right, but that dung hole was even worse. At least he could refuse to go into the dung hole.

"Well, we got a place for you," the warden said, nodding to the guards. "Number eight," he said.

Victor was too tired to be terrified.

The guards dragged him to a harbour-facing room high in Rockhead Prison. They removed all of the glass from the windows. It was winter. He could see his breath when they shoved him in and slammed the door on his airy dungeon.

There was no mattress, just one ratty horsehair blanket laid on the floor.

There was no coat, no shutters. Nothing but prison and fresh air. Fresh, frozen air.

Victor fell asleep, glad at least to be away from the rats. He woke up shivering. The wind dropped deeply below zero as it blasted in from the ocean and huddled in his cell. It was like a walk-in freezer. It was like a morgue. He had to brush the snow off in the mornings. For breakfast and lunch, he got birdseed and water. Sometimes he got potatoes and cabbage.

What a feast!

This was number eight.

When it was time for exercise, the guards locked him alone in a long corridor and gave him free run of it. He didn't run, though. As soon as the guards left, he'd climb up the bars and look down into Africville, watch his friends running home from school. Tears streamed down his face.

One day, another boy climbed the hill of Africville and met Victor at the barred window.

"Eddie!" he said, grinning.

"Hey Victor," Eddie said, clinging to the bars. "I got you something."

Eddie reached into his pocket and pulled out a handful of chocolate bars. He carefully passed them through to Victor, who gobbled one and stashed the rest in his pocket.

"Thanks," he said through his chocolate-stained mouth.

Eddie grinned. "Clean the chocolate off your face," he said.

Victor nodded. Licked his face clean.

Happy thirteenth birthday, Victor Carvery!

He spent another year in Rockhead before being suddenly, inexplicably, released. His weeping mother met him at the front door and rushed him to safety at his grandfather's house in Liverpool.

22

Seaview United Baptist church was singing the roof off in the summer of 1960. The small sanctuary was packed. Everyone in Africville was there to see the baptisms, singing songs that skipped along the shimmering Basin and ricocheted off the hill. Eddie sat there in white, transfixed by heaven. Eddie felt good in church, unintimidated, at home. The church was the heart and lungs of Africville.

The church couldn't always afford a preacher, but they had Reverend W.P. Oliver today, assisted by Deacon Ralph Jones. Oliver talked about the hard world outside Africville, about how forbearance was required, about how you needed to be strong and humble.

"In the testing times, that is the time that we need that same God, and we feel that it is coming very handy. For men is waxing worse and worse. And friends, I want to say that if there was ever a time you want to stand by your God, it's now. Together we stand, divided we fall," preached Deacon Jones.

"Be like the willow. Bend, but don't break," preached Reverend Oliver.

Eddie breathed these words in like a deep-sea diver breaking for air.

The Carvery house had been bustling till late last night as his mother, grandmother and half of Africville prepared food and clothes for his baptism. It wasn't just him, though. His father Clarence, Aunt Emma, Elsie Desmond and his friend Gary Steed were all getting baptized.

Eddie's eyes were bloodshot and he was having a hard time staying awake. He hadn't been sleeping lately. He was afraid to close his eyes.

"I don't want to sleep," he whispered to his mother as she sat with him in the darkness of midnight. He could hear his brothers and sisters breathing.

It was the dreams. Night after night, Eddie was plunged into wild danger, his life nearly blown away in an extraordinary range of ways. He'd wake up in his mind, but not in his body, and so see the world paralyzed through a prism of dreams. He'd be walking down the road out of Africville, heading into trouble. Night after night, Eddie saw murder, mayhem and destruction. A world pulled into pieces. Drugs smashing men like wrecking balls through condemned houses. And night after night, the man with the big coat, hat and salt-and-pepper hair would save him, would sit with him and tell him things. Tell him wonderful things, about the ways of men and the true ways of God. The deep reality hidden behind the thin veil of perception. The man didn't look like Jesus, but Eddie knew it was him. He guided Eddie to safety. Protected him. Comforted him.

Eddie's dreams were discussed in church. He was born with the veil, so people paid attention to the workings of his soul.

The preacher led Eddie and the others down to Tibby's Pond, the edge of Africville and the earth's ocean. All those to be baptized wore dazzling white robes. Everybody else sported their finest. It was a long walk, a walk down the same road his grandfather and his great-grandfather had walked in their day.

Usually, there were two camps in Africville, those who went to church and those who did not. People who liked to drink, gamble and party did not go to church and the church-goers rarely drank, gambled and partied. But everyone respected the church and everyone knew it was their church. On days like today, everybody came. People came from Preston and Hammonds Plains to see their kin baptized in Christ. White people from Halifax even drove by, slowing down to marvel at the sight.

The congregation reached the shoreline, songs rising up over the hill like doves. Bedford Basin glittered golden in the midday sun.

The initiates stood at the water's edge, filled with serene pride. Hundreds of people lined the shore, rising up on a jutting of land for a better view, clustered out on the rocks like cormorants. One by one, the white-hatted initiates were helped into the open water and walked out to the reverend. A lone man's voice sang out loud: "Hallelujah! I am saved by God."

The minister held them, prayed over them, lowered them back-first into the water.

Africville watched as Eddie rejected Satan and accepted Christ.

The spirit of Africville flickered in the air like northern lights.

Songs called for God's strength.

Eddie beamed as he walked back to land, feeling the Lord working deep within him, feeling an impenetrable shield descend around his soul.

At the huge celebration that followed, all that food was gobbled up in no time.

23

Eddie landed a job on a seal-hunting ship heading north when he was sixteen. The money was good, plus it was his first chance to get out of Nova Scotia – and school. Victor, fourteen and freshly out of jail, jealous of his older brother's coming adventure, walked down to the wharf to see him off. Eddie was excited, head filled with high-seas adventures.

"Hey, you guys need an extra guy?" Victor optimistically asked a big blond sailor sitting on the pier.

"No, I only need one guy," he replied in thickly-accented English. "Just you."

"Hey, I was here first!" Eddie protested. "I was here first. He's my brother – he's just seeing me off," he explained.

"I want to go seal-hunting too. I need money," Victor argued.

"Well, I don't need two men," the sealer said. "I'll tell you what I'll do. I'll flip a coin. Whoever wins the toss goes out."

The brothers looked at each other. Nodded.

The sealer flipped the coin.

Victor won.

He grinned and boarded the *Minia*, waving to Eddie as it pulled out of the harbour.

There were eight crew on the ship, tall, blond Norwegians who spoke little English and couldn't pronounce Victor's name.

"Is okay if we call you Blackie?" asked the old man running the ship.

Victor thought about it. Being an Africvillian, he was used to abuse, to being called out of his name, but he could see the sailors had no racist intent, just ignorance.

"Sure," he agreed.

Victor was the galley boy, working below deck as the ship chugged north. He helped the cook, served food and cleaned up. He had no desire to kill anything, let alone a brown-eyed seal, but when he started to see the black tags the sealers were racking up, he changed his mind. Each tag was worth money: $30, $50, even $1,000. His mother could use that kind of money.

"Can I go out there so I can get some of those?" he asked the captain as the ship pushed its way through the ice fields.

"No," he said, "you're not a hunter."

The captain turned away from the boy to do some work.

The boy popped round in front of him.

"Well, you can teach me to be a hunter," Victor countered. "Show me what to do. Let me drag that hook out to those guys and bring the pelts in. I'll start like that."

"No, no, no, no, no!" the captain said. "It don't work like that, Blackie. It don't work like that."

"Well, how does it work?" Victor asked.

The captain rolled his eyes at the eager boy-hunter before him and walked off, raising his hands to warn the boy from following him.

Victor followed. He pestered the captain for days.

"Okay, okay, Blackie!" the captain finally yelled, throwing his hands up in defeat. "You win. You become big hunter," he said, laughing.

He agreed to put Victor on the ice. This is how it worked: the ship put down a plank, which skimmed over the ice floe as the ship sailed along. When the plank landed on a solid chunk, the hunter would run down it, club in hand. On the ice, he'd hunt seals until the ship returned. Easy.

The captain gave Victor a club, knife and gloves. Victor wore his sneakers and overalls – that's all he had. He was dressed for Africville, not the Arctic. The captain told him he'd freeze to death, but Victor insisted he'd be fine. He imagined the ship would only be gone a little while. How cold could it be?

Victor got up at the crack of dawn on Seal Day. He served breakfast to the other men and got into all of his clothes, grabbed his club, knife and pole, and stood jumping with excitement at the side of the ship. Jumping to stay warm, too. He hadn't spent much time on deck. Turns out it was colder than the kitchen. Victor was so wound up he didn't pay it any mind. A couple of hunters raced down the plank to start work. Then it was Victor's turn. He was on the plank leaning over the side of the ship when a car-sized cake of ice flowed past the ship, bumping against the wood.

"Jump, Blackie, jump!" the captain hollered from the deck as Charlie, Victor's hunting partner, leapt ashore.

"I ain't jumpin'!" Victor protested as the ice whizzed past. He got off the plank and ran back on the ship, staring at the other hunters with wide eyes, like they'd somehow betrayed him.

The other hunters fell about themselves laughing at him.

Charlie was rapidly fading from view, looking back at the ship and shaking his head.

Victor took a deep breath, got back up on the plank and readied himself, eyes peeled for a good chunk of ice.

"Jump, Blackie, jump!" the old captain shouted as one whizzed by, but Victor stayed put.

The old man cursed at him, shaking his fist menacingly.

"I'll jump! I'll jump!" Victor protested, trembling with fear and excitement.

Another floe.

"Jump, Blackie, jump!" shouted the captain and everybody else on board who wasn't in hysterics with laughter.

Victor glanced up at the captain and saw a rifle pointed right at him. It was used for shooting seals from the bridge, but was currently aimed at a little Black boy.

Victor jumped. His sneakers hit the ice and flew over his head, crashing him down into a pool of ice-cold water. Victor burst out of the liquid like it was electrified and sprinted after the departing ship.

"Wait! Stop the ship! I want to get back on!" he hollered. The ship kept on going, and the hunters were laughing over the edge. Victor ran for ages before giving up.

The ship was gone.

Victor was all alone on an ice floe in northern Canada.

All he could see was white snow and ice. It was eerily quiet; only the creaking ice and crunching snow broke the silence.

He headed back toward where he'd last seen Charlie. Victor was soaking wet and the icy wind soon froze his clothes. By the time he caught up to Charlie, his coveralls were solid ice so he had to walk like a robot. His little goatee was full of icicles and his bushy hair was hoary white.

Charlie looked up at him. The blond man shook his head.

"Today, Blackie, you die," he said.

Victor stared at him.

He looked all around him.

All he could see was ice.

"Okay," he said, voice shaking.

He understood it wasn't a death threat, just a statement of fact.

He started dancing around to keep warm, but it didn't work. They had a whole eight hours to kill before the ship passed their way again. Victor cuddled with a snowbank, imagining he was snuggling into the chesterfield in his house. He thought he heard his mother calling to him from deep within the floe.

"Keep moving, Blackie," Charlie said, driving the boy on as they searched for seals. "Not a seal in sight," he muttered.

Victor smelled a very familiar smell. His head perked up and Charlie cocked an eye at him. Victor ran the smell through his brain. He knew it. It was way out of place. It smelled like …

"Africville!" he shouted, grinning. "I smell Africville!"

Charlie looked at him like he was crazy, but Victor knew what his nose was telling him. He leapt up on a shelf of ice.

"I can smell it!" he hollered, eyes scanning the horizon.

"Victor crazy!" the Norwegian said to the vast Arctic wilderness, circling his finger around his ear.

"No! I can smell it!" Victor insisted. "Come on! Down over here!"

He sprinted off, slipping and sliding on the ice, falling and getting back up, Charlie reluctantly running behind.

Victor came over a hill and stopped, the familiar scent flooding his nose. Before him sprawled an endless field of thousands of seals.

He grinned.

"It smells like Africville," Victor said to himself, "like the seal abattoir in Africville."

Victor was just about an iceberg himself by then, his skinny limbs shivering out of control. He ran down into the seal herd, ripping off his frozen clothes as he went. When he reached the seals, he was as naked as they were. His eyes iced. His blood stopped. His skin cracked.

He bonked a seal on the head with his club, avoiding looking into its big, innocent eyes.

"It's either you, bud, or me," he stuttered through his clattering teeth as the seal fell over.

He slit the animal open and hot blood gushed out. He grabbed handfuls and rubbed it all over his naked skin. It was as warm as a bath, so he killed three more seals and slathered their blood over his bony body. He cut a few skins off and wrapped himself in pelts. He made himself seal shorts, seal shoes and a seal jacket, basking in the borrowed heat.

He killed another seal, washed himself in its hot blood and made pant legs. All you could see was his eyes. He was Sealman.

Huffing and puffing, Charlie finally caught up and gasped when he saw enough seals to fill up the whole fleet.

He gasped again when he saw the bipedal seal monster.

"It's me, Charlie, Victor," the boy said, pulling the seal mask down to show his face. Charlie's eyes popped. It was still cold, so Victor pulled the skin back over his skin.

Charlie went to work and they were still at it when they heard the ship blowing its horn, calling her hunters home.

"Go tell them we here," Charlie instructed.

Victor bounded off and waved as he ran to the ship. The men pulled up the hook in a panic when they saw a crazed seal spirit running at them and the ship started to speed away, the men on the deck staring in horror.

Victor waved and shouted, pulling the skins off his face to show it was him.

He finally convinced them.

"Blackie!" they shouted.

All of the hunters came ashore and went to Victor's field of seals. They slaughtered all their vessel could hold, leaving thousands behind.

The ship ended its long sojourn up north and sailed south to Halifax.

24

Victor burst into his house, grinning. His mom was in the kitchen; Eddie was in the living room.

"Eddie!" she said, wrinkling her nose. "What's that stinking smell?"

They both went to the door and jaws dropped at the cocky boy standing in the doorway, stinking like seal corpses.

Victor held up two coat hangers full of black tags. More made a necklace around his neck.

"We're rich!" he cried.

His mother smiled, hugged her stinking boy, and took him up to the bath.

The next morning, Victor ran down to the shipping company to collect his earnings. He beamed at every person he passed and they grinned at him. All of Africville had come by the party last night to celebrate his safe return.

He noticed the sealing ship was gone.

He went up to the company's office. The woman at the front desk directed him to a man in a dim office.

The man peered at Victor over his desk and said he'd never heard of him. He got up and shut the door in his face.

How much money did Victor collect from his seal-hunting adventure? Not a penny.

He dragged his feet back to Africville.

25

Eddie dropped out of school when he turned sixteen. He – and Mrs. Beck – had made it to grade seven. It was 1962 and there was no work in Africville anymore. The future was grim. The City was already knocking down houses and businesses, singing foreboding songs about relocation and renewal. Eddie's mother, Daisy, protested with all her breath, attending the showy public meetings where white City folk made concerned faces and listened to the Black people of Africville. The decision to demolish the village had already been made, but consulting still seemed important to the City.

In a distant TV studio, John Edward Lloyd slicked back his wavy salt-and-pepper hair, did up his tie and explained to the world how it was. He was the mayor of Halifax and so he knew. "Africville, obviously, must be redeveloped," he said, seated, looking down at the unseen TV reporter. "And sometimes, some people need to be shown that certain things are not in their own best interests and not in the best interests of their children. Now you do this – you want to take these projects certainly by persuasion," he went on, making a concerned-daddy face. "Rather certain, you don't coerce people against their will, but should there be violations of minimum standards, then you have no alternative but to enforce the law, and this is universal for everybody."

In Africville, Leon Steed told a reporter how it was. "The folks up here have been going to the City to find out about the roads, the lights, the garbage and what's the use? It made no difference," he said, squinting in the sunlight under his cap. "You see the condition of Africville today?" he asked, indicating the house in rough shape behind him. "This should have never been. If the City had took care of this place or say, help out, instead of been neglecting it, it would have been a lot better than what it is today."

In another interview, wearing a white sweater and sitting outside on a well, the sixty-three-year-old originally from Jamaica quoted an alderwoman in Halifax who had called his village a "scar on the face of Halifax."

"She was wrong there. Africville is not a scar; it's a sore," he said. "And who made it like that? The City."

He didn't want to swap his spacious home surrounded by green land for a rented apartment in the city.

TV crews and newspaper men and social workers were all over Africville. For years, it was one of the biggest running stories in Halifax – Canada, even.

"The City wants to redevelop it over our people and I don't think that's fair," said Joe Skinner, a big, sober man in a dark suit and tie with a white shirt. The CBC identified him as a railway porter. He sat on his sofa in his living room. His neighbour, Emma Steed, Leon's wife, sat at his side. The reporter asked them why they thought Africville had no running water, no sewage. Is it discrimination? he wondered. Is it because you're coloured?

Emma and Joe nodded, outlined the discrimination they'd faced on account of their dark skin.

"Frankly, I find this a bit hard to believe," the off-camera reporter said, before informing his hosts that their neighbourhood would make an excellent industrial site.

Joe swallowed anger and quietly stated his case. "I think we should have a chance to redevelop our property as well as anybody else. This is our property – it's been for the last two hundred years."

He told the reporter he didn't want to trade a home he owned for rented City property. "When you're in this country and you own a piece of property, you're not a second-class citizen," he explained. He paused, holding the reporter's gaze. "That's why my people own this land. They worked for it, they toiled for it, they worked to get this little piece of land that they own and they try to hang on. But when your land is being taken away from you and you ain't offered nothing, then you become a peasant in any man's country."

The reporter badgered the two Africvillians, saying surely with all this hard treatment, they hated white people.

"No, we don't hate them," Mrs. Emma Steed answered quietly, confidently. "We want to show we know all men is equal. We got that much sense to know the Lord made all men equal and he doesn't want us to hate one another."

The bulldozers weren't swayed. Houses continued to fall. No one wanted to leave Africville, but Africville was leaving them.

Okay, some people wanted to leave Africville. Can you blame them? They were promised a home for a home and all that plumbing, paved roads and dump-free land, plus education for their children, jobs and a handful of money. Sounded pretty good.

Eddie left, heading for Calgary. He'd always fancied himself a cowboy.

Eddie made it to Montreal, where he met up with two older guys he knew from Africville. He stayed with them a bit, but then the young, angry men trashed their rented accommodations and disappeared. Another roommate told Eddie to get out of there before the cops came to arrest him, so he left Montreal.

Eddie walked west, thumb out, and a car soon stopped. Eddie looked in to see a friendly white face.

"You going west?" Eddie asked.

The driver nodded.

"My mother's in the hospital in Ottawa," the driver explained. He was travelling from his home in Kingston, Nova Scotia, to see her and offered Eddie a lift as far as the capital.

Eddie climbed in the vehicle. The Annapolis Valley boy didn't know much about Africville, but was keen to listen to Eddie's stories.

Down the road, they saw two more men hitchhiking. Eddie recognized them – it was the two Africville guys who trashed the place in Montreal.

"Do you know them?" the driver asked.

"Yeah, they're from Africville," Eddie answered.

"It's like an exodus!" he joked, slowing down. He stopped the car and welcomed them into the Africville Express.

"Where are you fellows going?" he asked, smiling to the back seat.

"Toronto," answered the older one.

The two guys filled him in on their travels, leaving out the trashing in Montreal.

"Tell you what I'll do," the driver said. "I'll take you guys to Toronto, but then I've got to go back to Ottawa to see my mother."

The two guys exchanged a look that made Eddie uneasy.

They arrived in Toronto late that night. The two guys led the driver to a rough part of town where the city was tearing down buildings.

"Here?" he asked, incredulous. "This place is falling apart!" But then, his mind freshly filled with stories of dumps, disease hospitals and demolitions, he thought maybe this was the Ontario version of Africville.

The two guys got out of the car.

"Yeah, this is home. Come on out. There's something I want to show you," one said.

The driver hesitated, then opened his door and got out. Eddie stayed in the car.

The older guy grabbed the driver and the younger bashed him over the head with a rock. As he fell, they fell on him.

"No! No! Don't do it. This is wrong. This is a guy from Nova Scotia, he's doing us a favour!" Eddie protested from the front seat. The bigger of the two men glared at Eddie. Skinny and scared, he didn't dare leave the car.

They kicked and beat the Valley man until he stopped moving, then rooted through his pockets and took his wallet and watch.

They got back in the now-stolen car and drove in silence to a friend's house, leaving the driver unconscious on the deserted street. When they explained their predicament to their Toronto friend, he agreed to put them up for the night.

Early in the morning, the guys left, warning Eddie to stay put.

At noon, the police burst in the front door and swarmed the apartment. The Valley man had lived and helped police track down his assailants. Eddie was the only guy there, so they arrested him.

"We already caught your two friends," one officer said as they handcuffed him and dragged him to the squad car.

"I didn't do anything wrong," he protested as they drove him to the station. "I know I was there, but I couldn't help it. I was in the car."

The police ignored him.

Eddie got twelve months in jail, with a possible further ten months. The cops in Ontario called the cops in Halifax, who said Ontario could keep Eddie as long as they liked. They were busy knocking down Africville.

In jail, Eddie resumed the education that had stopped in grade seven. He learned sheet metal from an expat Englishman called Hughes. Hughes had a furnace parts business and came into the prison to teach guys like Eddie everything he knew.

Eddie started reading and writing and mastered math. He quickly caught on to drafting and was soon a qualified sheet-metal worker. After so many years of Mrs. Beck, he was surprised to find out he wasn't stupid after all.

He also found trouble had a way of following him.

26

The prison guards manhandled Eddie past the cells, throwing him down the Hole. He crashed into the wall, hitting it chin first. Vicious pain flared through him and he fought back a scream.

The Hole door slammed shut.

Eddie sat alone in the dark, his jaw searing with pain. His past was a blacked-out disaster and his future a bombed-out war zone.

He had wound up in the Hole after smashing a French guy from Northern Ontario in the face. They had been friends, but other inmates pressured him into calling Eddie a nigger. It was a bad day for a bad decision. Eddie had a toothache, his grandfather had just died and he was angry with himself for missing the funeral in Africville. And then this dope, who used to be his pal, goes and calls him out of his name like that. So Eddie pounded the guy, the other inmates pounded him, then the guards broke them up and then the guards pounded Eddie and threw him in the Hole.

The swollen, abscessed tooth he'd been ignoring got worse in solitary confinement. He had complained so loudly the prison guards had yanked him out of the Hole and dragged him to the prison dentist. He sat Eddie down without even saying hello and hauled the tooth out, chatting to the guards about the hockey game last night.

"What's the point," Eddie mumbled to himself as his eyes adjusted to the darkness back in the Hole. He fell down, exhausted, head pressed against the dirty floor. He folded his arms around himself, shivering, trying to stop the chill. Family was gone, friends were gone, his childhood was a disintegrating memory one thousand miles away from this cell. He closed his eyes, wondering how he could kill himself in the dank, empty Hole.

The air changed.

The wall changed.

Eddie sat up. Opened his eyes.

The wall transformed, turned transparent, and suddenly Eddie was sitting in the happy warmth of Africville. It was the church and all the older people – his mother, grandmothers, aunts, uncles, cousins and friends – sat in well-lit pews in front of him. They held hymn books and sang the old songs to the Saviour.

The music reached Eddie's deafened ears, lifting his spirits. His strength grew as he watched the faces of those he loved, and who loved him.

Eddie suddenly realized he couldn't be there, and suddenly he wasn't. The light of Africville faded, the wall turned back to stone, and Eddie was back in the dark in the Hole in his johnny shirt.

His mind leapt to Peter, visited by angels in prison.

He stopped shivering.

It was time to go home.

He was a model prisoner after that, focused on getting out of prison so he could get back to Africville. The jailors didn't care about his prison vision, so he served the full twenty-two months before hitching his way back east.

27

Africville was being beaten to death. Hardly any buildings were left standing – some houses and the church. Everything else – and everyone else – was gone, bulldozed one after the other. Homes, businesses, shops, schools, halls: all gone. Sometimes the City paid $500 for a property, sometimes not. It depended on paperwork. Sometimes, like with Eddie's cousin Jim, they paid two people for the land. Neither of them was Jim, so neither had a deed, but the City bulldozed his house anyway. When Jim came angrily at them, waving his deed, they shrugged and explained they'd already paid twice and that was enough for any rotten shack. Jim turned icy, explained to them that it wasn't a shack but a fine house. They shrugged again.

The story was that the City was trading a house for a house, so that Africville would be urban renewed up in Halifax. But word spread that people were taking the $500 and being moved into condemned houses until a space opened up in Uniacke Square, a new public housing development being built in the North End of Halifax, about three kilometres south of Africville. You could rent there as long as you liked, but you couldn't buy. It was a home for a loan, equity exchanged for a lifetime debt to the City.

Some people fought. Pa Carvery wouldn't go, and neither would Granny Pink. Money meant nothing. They were old people who'd lived forever in their homes and had no desire to move. Just build around me. Just tear down around me. Leave me be.

Eddie's oldest brother Dickie was staying at Granny Pink's then, along with his new wife, their children and a daughter she had from a previous relationship. The girl, Stephanie Sparks, would sit with Granny Pink in the daytime and marvel at the beauty of the diamond-sparkling snow and the glittering lights on their neighbour's house until a train roared through, releasing black smoke to cloud everything.

Granny Pink and Stephanie sat in the post office and watched the houses being torn down during the day and during the night. They'd look out the window with grim faces, listening to the screaming and crying as another house was demolished. Some people lost everything, their houses plowed under with all of their possessions.

All the while, the ocean lapped against the back of the extension on Granny Pink's house, crashing at night like the waves wanted to eat the house. The noise of the water terrified Stephanie. The screaming from the displaced Africvillians chilled her heart. Everybody felt it when one of the corner stores went.

Eddie was around. Stephanie saw him as a mentor, though she knew he was wild. Who wouldn't be? She still liked him.

Old people talked about how it went when the City put train tracks through, first in the 1850s and again in the early 1900s. At the start, the City asked everyone nicely, explained how it was great news for Africville, how the City was making a really generous offer for the homes that stood where the City wanted the train tracks to go. Some accepted and left Africville or tried to find somewhere else to live in the village and others said no, thanks anyway, I'll stay put. Both times, the City bulldozed all of the homes. With that precedent set, the options a lot of people saw during the final demolition of Africville were 1) Take the $500 and lose your home; or 2) Refuse the money and lose your home.

So they took the money.

Sarah Mantley didn't take the money. She just went to visit her sister in Preston and came home to find her home had been bulldozed. She had no warning and so everything was crushed up together – her clothes, furniture, dishes. Everything, just levelled in a couple of hours, leaving her homeless. Nini Dickson took ill and was taken to the Dartmouth hospital. The City smashed her house down before she could check out. She came home to see everything she owned in a rained-on pile of timber. Neighbours, those who were left anyway, had rescued some of her things for her, but most everything was ruined. James Stewart was in the hospital, too, when the City snuck up and bulldozed his house. People were afraid to leave Africville. You'd go for a walk and come home to find your house half destroyed, a hungry bulldozer ramming into it until it fell down.

A moving company was contracted to help those who couldn't afford to rent a truck. It pulled out at the last minute, so the City provided an alternative. Bright yellow dump trucks were taken off the dump and made available to deported Africvillians. People stuffed whatever belongings they could onto the back of the dump truck and headed for the city. Their new neighbours watched behind lace curtains as the Africville diaspora unpacked dump trucks full of furniture. What else would you expect from the dump dwellers?

In the middle of one night, Dickie came staggering in the door of his mother's home, eyes wild, gasping for breath.

"The church is gone!" he hollered, and kept hollering until the whole house was awake.

"What is going on?" Daisy asked, cinching her housecoat as she came downstairs. She could smell the alcohol on her son.

"They flattened the church!" he repeated, like he was about to cry.

"It can't be, it can't be!" she said.

"It is, Mamma, right to the ground."

Eddie, Dickie and Daisy went outside to see the last of the City machines crushing the church, headlights flashing through the dark night of Africville. It was all gone – bell, tower, choir, organ, everything – reduced to a tangled pile of beams, pews, pulpits and crosses.

It was three a.m.

"You can't take the church," Dickie shouted. "The people ain't gone yet!"

"Yes, it's gotta come down," the City man said, not taking his eyes off the bulldozer.

Later that day, the City filled the church basement with rocks, so it couldn't be rebuilt. Pretty much everyone left then, except for Pa Carvery, Granny Pink and a few others.

The church had held its last service just a few weeks before, on Easter Sunday, 1967. Of course, no one knew they were holding the church's funeral service. Or did they? Maybe they knew. Because the hymn that rang through the old white church as a creeping red sun sawed through the grey clouds, the hymn that echoed off the green hills as people huddled into their dark coats in the damp spring chill, the hymn that skipped over the blue waters of the Basin and through the deserted streets of Africville as the remnants of its people clapped and sang, the hymn that filled the wooden church while Mrs. Deacon Jones laid into the piano, that hymn was an old Negro Spiritual called "You've Got To Move."

You've got to move
You've got to move
When our Lord speaks
You've got to move

Eddie's brother Irvine almost didn't move fast enough. He escaped the bulldozer by inches and seconds. He and some friends were playing in an old shed they used as a hangout. They were in it when a bulldozer smashed through the wall. The boys got to their feet and got running before they got killed. The driver laughed as they escaped.

Daisy Carvery had to move to a condemned house in the city. It was nice, and big, and she liked it fine, but it was slated to be demolished, so no one got too attached.

"They took our homes, they moved us out of Africville in the City garbage trucks," Daisy told a public meeting after she'd had to move. "We had a lot better out there than some places they put us in this city. They put us right in, a lot of us, right in the slums. The meanest part they did to Africville was they got the older people together – they didn't want to hear anything from the younger generation – because they simply knew the older people didn't have any education. What is five hundred dollars to a seventy-five-year-old Negro? He thinks he's rich! What can he do? We haven't even got enough to put down one payment for a home. Nothing!" she said, raising her empty hands. "I'm living on welfare. I think a whole lot of us, when we came in this city, we had to go on welfare. When we lived in that city of Africville," she continued, pointing towards the vanished community, "you look in the records and see how many in Africville had to humble and come to the City for welfare. We were too independent. We didn't want it. We earned our own living and we earned it the honest way! Our boys never had so much trouble till they came in the city."

The City tried to find housing for all the displaced people, but who wanted a bunch of Black people coming out of the dump on garbage trucks? One group of white people in Halifax organized to pre-empt relocatees coming to their neighbourhood, arranging a protest around the theme "We don't want Africville people here."

Eddie lived with his father for a bit down by the site of the new bridge, but that house was soon taken.

"The whole thing in an eggshell was us," Clarence Senior, a balding old man with a dapper moustache, would later say as he smoked a cigarette. "We was all accumulated as one, because we were Black. That's the reason why the City wanted to get us out of there. That's the only one reason why."

Eddie went into Halifax. He had vague ideas of life working out there, of getting a job, getting a girl, getting that house for a house, and having that nice life he saw others having.

He even landed an interview with the one sheet-metal company in Halifax. He dressed up and took his draftings along. He sat down across from the boss's desk and explained what his skills were.

"Nah, it'll never happen," the boss said, waving him quiet. "You're the wrong colour. I don't want no Black people working in my company."

He explained it wasn't a racist thing. It was just that it would upset the other workers and screw up his whole business. Nothing personal. You understand.

Eddie left, throwing his portfolio in the trash on his way. He walked back to Africville. The dump was still there, so Eddie went back to work, his anger burning like a mountain of toxic trash.

28

When Rocky Jones and his friends stepped off the plane in Halifax, Rocky's jaw dropped. There were police everywhere. He looked behind him to see what celebrity, criminal or political leader had been on their flight, triggering the massive response of armed, unarmed, uniformed and uninformed officers that had taken over the usually quiet airport.

"Look at all the cops! I wonder who they're here for," he said as his wife and their friends went to collect their bags. His friend, an American named Stokely Carmichael, shook his head. Stokely's wife, Miriam Makeba, shrugged her shoulders. The police cameras started flashing. They were all flashing at Rocky and Stokely.

"Oh shit, I think they're here for us!" Rocky said. "Fuck. What's going on?"

"I don't know, man. Let's just get out of here," Stokely said, warily watching the cops watching him. Official faces followed their every move. The RCMP had been bugging Rocky's phone for years and knew every step of the planned visit. Rocky and Stokely grabbed their bags, jumped in a car and headed for the city.

It was October 1968. Rocky Jones was a Black man born in Truro, Nova Scotia, who had long since left home and developed a global perspective on the racism he had been born into. Here's how deep it went: when he moved to Halifax, he went to see a dentist because his tooth hurt. A Black man walked into the dentist's office and hovered over young Rocky, tools in hand.

"Uh, it doesn't hurt so much, actually. I think I'll just go," Rocky said, sliding out of the chair and out of the office.

Rocky had never seen a Black dentist. He couldn't even imagine a Black dentist. He thought this man was an imposter.

So when Rocky grew up and learned how the world works, he became a big fan of Stokely Carmichael. Stokely was the honorary prime minister of the Black Panthers Party for Self-Defence. He birthed the idea of Black Power.

"It is a call for Black people in this country to unite, to recognize their heritage, to build a sense of community. It is a call for Black people to define their own goals, to lead their organizations," Stokely explained after being arrested on a march with Martin Luther King Jr. in 1966.

Stokely introduced the world to the idea of "institutional racism."

When Stokely Carmichael rolled into Halifax, Malcolm X had been dead three years. Martin Luther King Jr. had been dead six months. In the wake of King's April 1968 assassination, race riots had burned across one hundred American cities. Stokely was at the centre of the Washington, D.C., riot, which started with him asking shopkeepers to close out of respect for the slain civil rights leader. The fighting flared into April 5, when U.S. President Lyndon Johnson called in federal troops. Twelve people died and one thousand were injured. In South Africa, the homeland of Miriam Makeba, Nelson Mandela was four years into his long walk on Robben Island. In Halifax, Africville was in its death throes.

A lot of people saw Stokely as a new *Mont Blanc*, sailing into Halifax with an explosive cargo.

"Our grandfathers had to run, run, run. My generation's out of breath. We ain't running no more," Stokely said in a 1967 speech quoted in a *Life* magazine article headlined "Whip of Black Power." "Where in God's name do we exercise any control, as a people whose ancestors were the proudest people who walked the face of this Earth? Where? Where, I ask you? Everywhere he's gone, he controls our people. In South Africa, he steals the gold from our people, in the West Indies, he steals the material from our people. In South America, where he scattered our people, he's raping us blind. In America, he rapes us. In Nova Scotia, he rapes us!"

He sneered at the ideas behind integration.

"We were never fighting for the right to integrate. We were fighting against white supremacy. 'Integration' as a goal today speaks to the problem of Blackness not only in an unrealistic way but also in a despicable way … 'integration' is a subterfuge for the maintenance of white supremacy."

The Black Panthers were armed and led by a man called Huey P. Newton.

"My name is Huey P. Newton. I'm minister of defence of the Black Panther Party. I'm standing on my constitutional rights. I'm not going to allow you to brutalize me. I'm going to stop you from brutalizing my people. You got your gun, pig, I got mine. If you shoot at me, I'm shooting back."

That's how Newton, the "baddest motherfucker ever to set foot in history," confronted corrupt cops in the ghettos of America, according to his friend and fellow Panther Bobby Seale in his book *Seize the Time: The Story of the Black Panther Party*.

Stokely agreed.

Rocky agreed.

"You name the weapon and I'll meet you," Rocky would say. "If you want to have a spelling bee, well, I'll be there spelling to challenge you. If you want to be intellectual and debate, I'll be intellectual and debate. But if you want to go to war, I'm prepared to put my body on the line and go to war."

When Stokely and Rocky met at a Black writers' conference in Montreal in the fall of 1968, they clicked. Jones took a look at the besieged, passionate, articulate intellectual and realized one thing: the man needed to chill out.

"You need to take a break from all of the real action," Rocky told Stokely. "Why don't you come to Halifax to chill? Halifax is a pretty laid-back place. It's like Boston. We can go fishing. You can stay at my house."

Stokely wasn't sure. Rocky sold him on the blue water and green fields. Come to Nova Scotia. Come to life. Bring your wife.

His wife was Miriam Makeba, the world-famous South African folk singer and anti-Apartheid civil rights fighter. They had just gotten married. Her U.S. record deals and concerts had just been cancelled.

Stokely thought it over and agreed to follow Rocky home. On the flight, Rocky told him more about schizophrenic Halifax. It looked peaceful, but racism roiled under the surface. The racism was overt and it was covert. There was a huge race problem, but most people thought there was no race problem. "You guys can stop by Preston. Meet some folks who would be honoured to know you," Rocky said. "Check out the fishing holes. Nothing political."

And then the police met them at the airport. Stokely checked out the tree-lined view as they sped into town, cop cars in tow.

"Hey, brother," Stokely said. "We can't organize a revolution around a car accident."

Rocky puzzled it for a moment. Slowed down.

Another fleet of armed cops was waiting for them at Rocky's house.

"Let's go out," Rocky suggested after they'd settled in. "Let's get a drink and something to eat."

Stokely nodded. "Sure. Where to?"

"I know the perfect place," Rocky said. They headed to the Arrows Club. Rocky knew the owners. When they pulled up, the police were already there – plainclothes cops sitting in cars outside, uniformed cops standing on the sidewalk and squad cars riding by. Police snipers patrolled nearby roofs, rifles out.

The fear in the city was palpable. The fear, Rocky thought, was the knowledge that its Black people were mistreated. The fear was that Black people may retaliate for that mistreatment. As Rocky saw it, the carefully crafted language of urban renewal, of social improvement, of integration, was blown away, revealing the race struggle at the heart of the destruction of Africville.

In the streets of Halifax, some white people imported guns from the States. Just in case.

The Jones party of four made its way into the packed Arrows Club. Word had spread and everyone wanted to meet the legendary leader who had so stirred up Halifax. It was a mixed-race club, so white and Black people came to say hello, to tell Stokely what they thought of his ideas. It was cordial, but non-stop.

"Can you please keep these crowds away from us?" Stokely asked the owner, Billy Downey. Billy was clearly stressed out.

"Look, we're just chilling. Don't worry – we're not here for anything other than to have a drink and a bite to eat and just meet the people," Rocky said. Billy roped off a section for them. People kept crowding in, sharing their thoughts.

Eddie Carvery entered the club and walked over to listen. He'd heard about Stokely and wanted to see him for himself. People told Stokely he was just what Halifax needed, or he was the last thing Halifax needed, as he ate his dinner.

They talked about King and "Beyond Vietnam," the landmark speech he made on April 4, 1967. It moved his mission from civil rights to poverty, workers' rights and a call for an end to the war in Vietnam.

"Martin Luther King begins to look at the garbage workers," Rocky said. "He begins to realize that the civic workers – which are not just Black workers, but all workers – that they have power and that they need to exercise their power. That's when he became dangerous and had to be killed. He began to move from viewing things strictly as a Black-white issue into looking at, 'Oh, there are some class issues here.' Well, here's this man that's got this huge following, this huge appeal, and now he's really prepared to take on American hierarchy with a whole different viewpoint. 'Boom. Up against the wall, motherfucker.' He had to go. That's why Malcolm X had to go."

"How do you feel about King's non-violence?" a man asked.

"There are a lot of people who grew up in the ghettos of North America who couldn't just turn the other cheek. They didn't know about Ghandi's philosophy of non-violence, about Martin Luther King's philosophy of non-violence, nor did they buy into it," Rocky answered. "That's not to say it's racist towards white. It's a reaction to an oppressive state power."

"So can white people help you?" a white woman asked.

"If you want to help me, don't come into my community to do things for me or to give me advice. Go to the person who's got his foot on my neck, talk to him, fight with him, because that's where you've got to be," Rocky said. "Don't bother me and my Black community. If you're white, you've got to take the struggle into the white community. If you are truly revolutionary, if you really want to do something in the struggle, then you got to go into your own community and organize. If I'm on the ground and someone's kicking the shit out of me, don't talk to me! I'm on the ground. Go to the person who's kicking the shit out of me and grab him!"

"Say, Miriam, will you sing us a song?" a man asked in a lull in the conversation.

She was hesitant. This was supposed to be a quiet break. She exchanged glances with Stokely.

"Okay," she agreed, smiling. Local legend Lottsa Poppa joined her for a song. Then another. The entranced crowd wanted more. Forty minutes later, Miriam Makeba and the band Four Hundred Pounds of Soul left the stage to thunderous applause from the Black and white crowd.

Stokely did a quick radio interview with a Dartmouth reporter. The story was all over the airwaves. The Black Panthers were in town.

Eddie listened for a bit, then headed back outside, glancing up at the police snipers who were glancing down at him. He noticed nearby businesses had been boarded up. Just in case.

"No," Eddie said to his friend as they headed back to Uniacke Square. "This is Canada. That's not the way we do it in Canada. We need to integrate. Don't kill Whitey. Go to bed with Whitey and we'll have mulatto children."

His friend laughed.

Stokely left the next day after an eighteen-hour stay. Back at the airport, a newspaper reporter caught up with him. "We recognize all the problems of Halifax that Black people have and we wanted to begin some co-ordination so that we can move against racism and capitalism," he told the journalist before catching a plane back to the States.

Halifax breathed out.

The city hadn't burned down.

Yet.

29

Eddie spent 1969 in Africville watching the last people move out. People were nervous, afraid and intimidated. The crushing weight of the City destroyed life. Africvillians were used to a sense of freedom, of autonomy, but the City trucks and City workers were everywhere now, finishing off the community. Social workers contorted their faces into a show of grief and explained how it was for the best. The ancient pact, the unspoken deal that had started between Halifax and the Maroons, was that Halifax would stay in Halifax, and Africville would stay in Africville. The pact was ruptured now and Black communities across Nova Scotia prepared to fight hard when their turn came.

Homeowners had struck small bargains with the City and thrown what possessions they could into the back of a dump truck, fleeing for whatever housing the City provided. Maybe it was for money, maybe a job, or maybe the promise of a good education for their children. Before they'd even got out of Africville, their home, the home to their families for generations, was bulldozed. This was a panic, an emergency evacuation. The bulldozers followed the exodus.

Granny Pink stayed and stayed. Dickie left with his wife and their kids and Stephanie. Granny Pink stayed. She watched her community being destroyed around her. Eddie went to the City and when he came back, she was still there in her lovely white house, with its lovely white picket fence, surrounded by the broken piles of her neighbours' bulldozed homes.

"It's my job to witness the demise of Africville," she told Eddie. It was palliative care. She loved Africville with all her soul, and she wanted to be there while it took its final breaths.

Granny Pink was tough, an old woman with her grey and black hair, but she was stronger than most of the young men and not easily moved.

"I don't want to go," she told Eddie as they stood on the now-empty stretch of dirt road.

Eddie was there when Granny Pink left. It was the last rites for Africville, an operation to remove its soul. Her two sons came with heavy, shame-ridden faces, and told her she had to go. The City was going to bulldoze her house, and might just do it with her inside.

Granny Pink didn't care. Let them bulldoze her.

"We've got you a nice home in town," they told her, tears stinging their eyes.

"I don't want to leave," Granny Pink said, crying, clutching her things as her sons loaded them into their vehicles. At least she was spared the dump trucks.

"I'm not going anywhere! You are wrong to do this," she said, unpacking the vehicles and trying to stop her sons. "This is my home and I do not want to go. This is the death of Africville."

Her sons kept stoic, kept packing, kept not looking at the ruins all around them. In the end, they had to pick their mother up and half-drag, half-carry her to the vehicle and pull her out of Africville.

A couple of days later, bulldozers flattened her house. She didn't last much longer.

Eventually, Pa Carvery was forced from the last home in Africville. He had no desire to leave his lifelong home. As Africville was bulldozed around him, he stayed. He was right in the path of the new bridge, though, and the City was bleeding money every day he stayed in the way of progress.

One cold day in December, 1969, the City summoned Pa Carvery to its downtown chambers.

"They sent for me and when I got there, I was taken into someone's office. There was five or six people in the room," he later recalled. The City solicitor, director of finance, the internal auditor, the social planner, someone called the Africville Special Projects Officer and two plainclothes cops were waiting for him. "Plus, a suitcase full of money tied up neatly in bundles. The suitcase was open and stuck under my nose so as to tempt me and try to pay me off right then and there. I didn't like it at all. It hurt me. I told them, 'You guys think you're smart … well, you're not smart enough.' Then I got up and walked out of the office."

The City knocked his house down anyway, on January 2, 1970. He got a bit of money. Less than that dirty offer, but at least he had a clear conscience. Pa Carvery stood in the ruins of his life, feeling like the City had stolen his heart right out of his chest, while a newspaper photographer took his picture.

The operation to destroy Africville wound up costing $800,000. Funnily enough, that was how much the City estimated it would cost to put in sewer lines, install running water and pave the roads. But saving Africville for $800,000 was way too expensive, so they went for what they said would be the $80,000 bargain of urban renewal. The City wasn't very good at guessing the cost of things, or the worth.

30

Eddie was living between Uniacke Square and the remnants of Africville. It was winter 1969 and the wastelands of Africville were turning white with frost and snow. In Halifax, Eddie had fallen for a pretty Black girl and she'd gotten pregnant, but her parents got wind of Eddie's prison past and quashed the relationship.

She had the baby and Eddie saw the little girl when he could.

He was sitting in the Rainbow Tavern one day when his brother Victor burst in, bleeding and wild. Eddie watched him grab man after man at the bar, looking for support for a fight. Victor had an ugly hole in his bottom lip and the teeth behind it were crushed. Blood poured out of his mouth. He looked like a vampire.

"You probably did it to yourself," man after man repeated, turning away. "You probably deserved it."

Victor had a bit of a reputation.

He found no takers, but then he found Eddie.

"You gotta help me!" he shouted. "I was walking to my ship on the jetty and when I walked past the building, those bastards hit me in the mouth with a spiked two-by-four!"

Eddie nodded, slipped off the bar stool. "We'll make it right. We don't need no gang. I'll go down with you and take care of these guys," he said, cracking his neck.

Politically, Eddie didn't believe in violence – hence his literal "make love, not war" approach to improving race relations. Personal violence was a different matter. He learned from a young age that you could radically alter a situation in your life just by hitting someone hard and so he often did.

Victor worked with fishermen, which meant any trouble was likely to be big trouble. The brothers stopped at Eddie's house so he could pick up his long dog chain. They also picked up a white relative who was staying there, an old, drunk guy from P.E.I. He had gotten shell shock fighting in Europe in the war and had never been the same.

A fight sounded like an enjoyable change from the routine and the trio walked to the Ocean Tavern.

It was packed. The drinkers were as white as they were Black at the Rainbow. Halifax didn't have those "Whites Only" signs that you saw in the States, but everybody knew which bars and restaurants were white only.

"Where's the guys who did this thing to you?" Eddie asked Victor, feeling that happy surge of violence in his veins.

"Up at the front," he answered.

The three men pushed through the crowd to the bar, drawing dirty looks.

"Where are they at?" Eddie repeated, eying up the men.

"Right here," Victor said, pointing to four big six-footers. The white guys stood up to answer the challenge. Eddie reached for his chain. One of the white guys grabbed his hand.

"You won't pull it out," he warned.

The guy was too close to hit and Eddie was surrounded, so he rammed his head into the guy's face. The man dropped Eddie's hand and slumped down against the wall. A fist smashed Eddie in the ear as he dodged out of the way. He spun to face it but a chair crashed over his head. He forgot about the fist and turned to the chair, but another guy punched Eddie in the back of the head. Dazed, he turned to face him, but another guy smashed a bottle on his head. Eddie forgot about the puncher and turned to the bottler.

The bar arranged itself into two rows and took turns pounding on skinny Eddie as he staggered from attacker to attacker. At first, he and Victor fought back-to-back but they were soon separated. Victor was gone and the old guy was nowhere to be found.

Eddie fought desperately to stay on his feet. There were a lot of boots on the ground and if he joined them, he'd never get up. He didn't want to die in the Ocean Tavern. He punched and kicked and scratched, threw bar stools, phone books and beer glasses. He battered a lot of white guys, but more kept coming.

The lines tightened into a circle, with Eddie in the middle. He tried to fight his way out, but every time he turned to face his attacker, someone else attacked him. He staggered in circles from beating to beating, trying to stay on his feet to at least keep from getting kicked to death.

A clearing opened up as the pack moved to a pool table. A big guy stood there, holding his cue, unhappy that his pool game had been interrupted.

Bleeding and battered, Eddie looked up. He knew the guy: Huey!

Eddie smiled.

"My man Hu – "

Huey cracked him over the head with the pool stick.

Skull split open, Eddie stared in horror as Huey charged him with the broken half of the stick, like it was a lance and they were two knights on horseback. Eddie grabbed it from him and tried to shove it through him, but the pack caught up and smashed another chair over his head. The gang beat him around the bar.

Suddenly a hand reached in, grabbed Eddie and pulled him out a side door.

"Come on!" said Victor, starting down the street.

Unbruised, unbleeding Victor.

Victor hauled Eddie down the street.

Eddie stopped still.

"Hold it! We can't leave the old man. We gotta go get him," he cried, wiping the blood out of his eyes. Steam was rising off his face as the hot blood encountered the cold air.

"Ah, he's white, they're not going to bother him. If you go back, they'll kill us," Victor said, pulling Eddie away from the tavern.

"No, that's not good enough," Eddie said, yanking his arm free and marching back to the bar. The drinkers were all setting things right, putting stools back and tending to the wounded. When they saw Eddie, everything stopped. The bar fell silent.

Eddie walked over to a scared-looking old man sitting on a stool at the bar. The old man was trying very hard to be invisible. Eddie touched him on the shoulder and he jumped.

"I'm okay. Let's go," Eddie said.

The bar parted to let them leave. Outside, Victor grabbed the old man's hand and they ran toward the North End.

"Come on!" Victor shouted to Eddie over his shoulder.

Eddie didn't move. He was thinking.

"No," he finally said. "I'm not going to leave it like that. I wanna finish this thing."

He imagined himself going back into the bar and enticing the fighters to chase him up to Gottingen Street, where he could find some backup to make it a fair gang war.

So he strolled back into the bar, blood gushing down his face and the world spinning. He wiped the blood out of his eyes and stood behind the glass partition, imagining it would keep him safe. He stuck his hand up and pointed over the glass at the drinkers, who stared at him in disbelief.

"You know what? Everybody?" Eddie shouted, head back, breath frosting in the wind. "All you guys in this tavern, everyone of yous put together, and you couldn't beat one little nigger!"

The bar blew up. A rain of pool balls battered the glass. It smashed, leaving Eddie open to whatever violence was coming his way. He turned and ran, pool balls cracking the back of his head as he fled.

A dozen fighters raced out after him, saw he was a half block away and still shouting at them.

They stopped, shook their heads and returned to the bar.

Eddie stopped, too, turned to the bar and shouted every awful word he knew. No one came out. His shoulders slumped. The adrenaline left.

That's when Eddie realized he was hurt. Dizzy, he started staggering along, wondering if he could get to home before he bled to death.

A huge freezer truck noisily braked beside him as he stumbled along Hollis Street, leaving a trail of blood.

"Hey," the driver yelled.

Eddie looked up.

It was one of the guys who had tried to kill him in the tavern.

He stared. At least the truck was something to hold onto.

"Get in the truck," the guy shouted.

"Are you crazy? You just tried to kill me. Now what are you going to do, take me in the truck and finish me off? Throw me in your meat freezer and serve me up to the City fathers?"

"Man, if you don't get in the truck, you're finished anyway. Look, I'm from Cape Breton and I just brought a load of fish up. I never witnessed nothing like that before. If you don't get in this truck right now and let me get you to the hospital, you ain't going to make it."

Eddie thought about it, thought the guy was probably right, and climbed up into the big rig. The Caper drove Eddie to the hospital and waited while the doctors stitched him up.

"Let's go to the police. I'll testify for you," he told a patched-up Eddie.

Eddie shook his head. It wasn't worth it.

"I just want to go home."

He thanked him and the two men went their separate ways.

31

Two weeks later, Eddie was still lying in bed, sleeping with bad dreams, when Victor burst in, shaking him awake. Eddie was slow to rise. His body and brain were battered from the brawl and he had barely moved in fourteen days. His mother had fed him, washed him, wrapped his wounds. This was the first he'd seen of Victor since the fight.

Their mother was right on his heels.

"Mom, I've got some work for Eddie. He can make $1,500," Victor said, shaking his older brother. "All he's got to do is go fishing."

Victor was working for a tug company, so he couldn't do it.

"Eddie, Victor got you a job," Daisy said to him.

The family was broke.

"Mamma, I'm hurt. I'm sick," Eddie protested, pulling a pillow over his head.

"That's okay," she said, pulling it off. "You can still be hurt and sick, but you can be on the boat."

Eddie stuffed a sea bag and hopped in a taxi to the South End docks with Victor. They arrived just before two a.m. The February water was icy and the ship was already leaving. Eddie ran out of the taxi and stopped at the edge, watching the ship go.

Victor was right behind him and shoved him over the edge. Eddie instinctively leapt into the boat to avoid the cold water. Eddie turned in shock and caught his sea bag as Victor threw it over.

Victor waved, shivering, and ran back to the taxi.

Eddie turned around to see fifteen white faces staring at him.

Every one of them had been in the Ocean Tavern.

The fishing trip was to last twenty-one days.

Some of the sailors laughed. Some snarled.

"You will not get back to shore," the leader growled as the boat churned out to sea. "We're going to leave you out there at sea."

Terrified, Eddie ran to the galley, kicked the door in and grabbed a skinning knife. He sharpened it and returned to the deck.

"Anyone who tries to do anything to me, I'm going to defend myself," he hollered, looking as crazy as he could. Crazy Eddie could look plenty crazy.

The men backed down, biding their time.

Eddie didn't sleep for two weeks. He worked all day and lay awake at night in his bunk, staring at the darkness, listening to the rumbling motor to stay awake. The knife never left his hand. He worked with it. He ate with it. He went to the toilet with it in his teeth. He sharpened it, looking as vicious as he could when another crewman passed.

The crew made throat-slitting gestures, dark comments about Davy Jones and the foreshortening of Eddie's life.

By day fifteen, Eddie was cracking up. He hauled himself out of bed after another sleepless night to take his position on deck. He went up the ladder, opened the hatch and had one foot on the deck when a voice called to him.

"Eddie," it said.

Eddie looked around. No one.

"Eddie," it said again.

No one.

Eddie continued onto the deck, but the voice stopped him again.

"Eddie," it said. "Down here."

He looked down.

It was a fish.

"Fish can't talk," Eddie said to the fish, who was lying with all the other fish in the hold.

"Oh yes we can," the fish said to him. "Eddie, throw me back into the sea. I've got a family."

The fish said that to Eddie, and Eddie said this to the fish: "I'm a fisherman. It's my job to come out here and catch fish to feed people."

Eddie felt ridiculous, talking to the fish.

"Please, I've got a family. Throw me back into the sea, Eddie," the fish pleaded.

Eddie hesitated. He looked at the fish. He looked out on deck. He looked back at the fish, which was staring at him with its big glassy eyes.

Eddie picked the fish up in his arms and glanced around, feeling awfully stupid. No one was looking. He slunk to the side of the ship and slid the fish back into the water.

"Thanks, Ed," the fish said as it swam away.

Eddie stared for a moment, then turned back to the boat, watching the crew take their positions.

He watched wearily as one man took his position at the side of the boat to haul in the heavy trawl door. The boat had one on each side and they both weighed as much as a car. The trawl doors were lowered into the water to trail the boat, anchoring the net and holding it apart like a pair of weighty wings. When the nets were full, the trawl doors were winched back on board and the man had to throw a chain around his door to prevent it from bashing into the boat. Eddie's job was to unload the fish.

Eddie watched as the man threw the chain, missed the hook on the trawl door, and instead caught himself on the edge of the boat, right in the path of the trawl door.

No one else saw the accident. Eddie wouldn't have seen it, but for the fish. He locked eyes with the terrified sailor. The ship defied physics and rolled right twice, keeping the trawl door away from the ship and giving Eddie time to run to the winch and grab a five-foot steel bar. Eddie jammed the bar into his stomach to hold off the massive door.

"Don't let go!" the sailor cried. The rest of the crew heard him and came, but stopped, frozen in dumbstruck horror. The ship rolled on the rough water, leaden grey skies pressing into black ocean.

"Help!" Eddie shouted at the mate, breaking his trance. The mate freed the trapped sailor and hauled him out of the way. Eddie leapt clear as the door slammed against the hull like the jaws of a monstrous crocodile just missing its prey. The steel rod sprang out of Eddie's stomach with a loud "ping!" and vanished into the night sky.

The crew gathered around Eddie.

Shaken, he backed up and held out his knife.

But the ship was all changed.

One by one, the men came up to Eddie and shook his hand. He kept the knife ready, just in case.

"You're a hero, man," they said. "You saved his life."

The men poured him a drink. They sat below deck, quietly reflecting on the brush with death.

The skipper offered Eddie a weekly stipend just to stay on board. He figured Eddie was some sort of good luck charm.

Eddie declined.

"I just want to go home," he said.

The crew understood.

Eddie got the rest of the shift off. He returned the knife to the galley, went to his bunk and slept for twelve hours.

32

Eddie and his mother Daisy would sit up late in her rented accommodation in Uniacke Square, talking about Africville. Where people had scattered to, how they were doing.

He could be a good listener, and he listened to his mother. After she left Africville, she lost her leg to diabetes. That took some of the fight out of her. Eddie sat with her often, talking, listening.

Daisy had battled hard against the relocation, rallying Africvillians to stop the City. She had organized meetings, talked to politicians and community leaders. Everyone listened with a concerned face, and then went back to what they were doing. She fought until she was all fought out.

After Africville, Daisy went to Liverpool to look after her father, who had taken ill. When she came back to Halifax, the family was staying in a house Clarence had gotten from the City. Evelyn went out to Liverpool. Clarence split soon after Daisy returned.

The house was a big place, big from when the rich people lived in that area. "Now we know how white people live," Eddie marvelled as he checked out the palace. It had a massive redwood hallway with hardwood floors, a grand staircase, high ceilings, rounded windows. It even had a dumbwaiter and servants' quarters. "This is a mansion."

It had been a doctor's house, but was now condemned. The pipes were frozen and the frame of the house falling down. It was good enough to house the Carverys for a couple of years before they got pushed up to Uniacke Square.

The new neighbourhood had a few shops, two restaurants, a tattoo parlour and a tavern called the Seaway. The tavern was a second home for Eddie. When he wasn't there, he'd be back out in Africville working the dump. His cousin Mannie was still there, and they still worked the dump together, though that came to an end soon.

Daisy encouraged Eddie to get a job in the city and he managed to land one with Mobren Cleaners. He started out working nights. That was fine with him, as it meant he could be in the tavern all day, drinking himself into a state where work seemed all right. Hard liquor mostly.

His mother dug into her new community in Uniacke Square. Straight away, she was fighting for crosswalks. She worked with people such as the boxer Buddy Daye to help start the North End Community Health Centre and the Ward 5 Neighbourhood Centre. Both opened their doors in 1971. Eddie was proud to see Daisy the Activist. But her heart was broken.

"They betrayed me," she said softly, her voice almost lost by the grind of the city outside the rented rooms in the Square. "Eddie, this is not a 'home for a home.' They promised us a home for a home. We owned that home. We paid our taxes. Now, we rent. We have nothing. They promised us royalties from the bridge, they promised us a road, they promised us a re-evaluation of the land. They sucked us in. They lied. They tricked us, and it was wrong, what they did. It was wrong and racist."

Daisy was angry, on the verge of tears.

"I want to make it right, Eddie," she said.

His mother had chosen Africville. Her mother was a Mi'kmaq medicine woman in Shubenacadie, and Daisy had passed those traditions on to Africville when she came with Eddie's father.

"When I first came to Africville, I fell in love with it. I started walking in at Duffus Street and just fell in love. It was so … beautiful," she said, her eyes fading as she looked at that faraway place. "The way the Bedford Basin sat, the view, the way the houses nestled."

She sighed heavily.

"You've got to do the protest," she finally said. "Irvine is a good boy, and he's doing his thing, but you've got to do your thing. You've got to clean up and do this."

She looked at Eddie, holding his hand.

"I'd go out myself, but I can't walk," she said. Wheelchairs were hard to come by, so she didn't go out much. When Eddie picked her up so she could go use the washroom, she cried. She tried not to, but the pain was too much. It broke Eddie's heart. It's the worst pain in the world, to hear your mother cry.

Eddie held her hand.

33

Eddie lay on his back in the grass burying the bones of Africville in the summer of 1970. Light clouds floated through the blue sky and a breeze from the Bedford Basin cooled the day. He drifted off and when he woke, a new flower had bloomed before his eyes. He walked over for a better look. It was the most beautiful flower he'd ever seen, but he had no idea what it was. He dropped to his hands and knees for a sniff. Glorious.

Eddie thought of his mother. She loved flowers. He'd pick it and take it into Uniacke Square to cheer her up.

He looked around to find something to hold the flower and came across a plastic bag. He started digging around the flower, planning to uproot the whole plant and take it into the city to replant it. He struggled with the roots, which went deep into the earth, wrapping around rocks. Eddie worked away at the flower, not noticing the darkening skies. Water-heavy clouds trundled across the heavens and the Basin churned up waves that nearly reached his feet. The wind whipped the sky and it bled rain. The storm battered Eddie.

He ignored it, focused on uprooting the flower. When it was out, he wrapped it in the plastic and stuffed it in his jacket pocket to protect it from the storm. He hopped on his bike and headed to town. Wind rammed against him, so it felt like he was pedalling just to stand still. Rain soaked his head and clothes. People scattered for shelter. He had the storm-drenched roads to himself.

Eddie made it to his mother's house in the Square and pulled out the flower, looking for a pot in which to replant it.

"Mamma," he said, shaking himself dry. "I want to show you this flower. I don't know where it came from, but it's beautiful. It just sprung up in the field and I thought that you should see it."

Daisy roused herself and watched her son open his jacket and pull out the plastic-covered flower. He removed the plastic.

The flower was dying. The petals were wilted and crushed. The stem drooped. The colours that had seemed so vibrant had paled.

Eddie was stung by the transformation.

"Eddie, you shouldn't have disturbed the flower," his mother said. "Take that flower back where you found it. It was only meant for you to see, so put it back."

"Yes, Mom," Eddie said, never one to disobey his mother.

He hopped back on his bike and headed for Africville, flower tucked back under his jacket. The skies stormed on and when he reached Africville, the Basin waves leapt out of the harbour and onto the grassy field. The wind bent the trees and fought Eddie. He struggled back into the field and found the hole. He put the flower back in the ground and scooped soil back over its roots.

The wind stopped howling. The rain stopped beating him. The water calmed.

"Sorry, flower," he said.

In time, the flower woke up and bloomed once more.

34

Later that summer, Eddie got hold of a beat-up tent and walked from Halifax to Africville. The houses were all gone, but still it felt like home. Foundations pockmarked the land like mortar shells in a war zone. City workers dragged the remaining carcasses of Africville's homes into the dump. They set it alight and burned the town they had once invaded.

Eddie walked to the edge of Tibby's Pond and pitched his tent. The City men glanced at him, ignored him. It wasn't unusual to see a Black person digging in the strewn garbage of the demolished community.

Eddie slept out there that night. The sound of Bedford Basin lapping on the shore of Africville soothed him and he awoke rested. It was good to feel solid earth under his body, to smell ocean air.

He stayed a while in Africville, then returned to the city. He had dim dreams of getting his life together, of landing a good job and maybe buying a house.

He learned about Africville's history. He started talking to the old people and reading books. He learned how the Coloured Hockey League was once the rival of anything Halifax's whites-only leagues could offer, bursting onto the scene with a brash, brazen style of play by pioneering flying body checks and inventing the slapshot. Most of the CHL players also played baseball, so the wind-up motion came naturally. Eddie Martin of the Halifax Eurekas is the man credited with inventing the devastating shot.

At the start of the twentieth century, the CHL drew huge crowds across the Maritimes, pouring money into the pockets of the Black entrepreneurs who ran it.

In 1906, the City wanted more Africville land, this time for the second set of train tracks. The owners of the property resisted, but the City went ahead anyway. Some of the resistant homeowners were the stars of the Africville Sea Sides, who used to practise on Tibby's Pond. The league stopped getting ice time in the rinks and had to move back outdoors. Newspapers stopped covering the matches. Eventually, the league died. The train tracks were built. Just a coincidence, of course.

Eddie learned how the City sent the Health Department to the Halifax Green Market in 1907. That was the place where Black and Mi'kmaq vendors had sold their fruit and vegetables to city folk for one hundred and twenty years. The Health Department pinched its nose, made a face, and said the market would have to go. The vendors were told they'd have to rent space in a new, white-controlled market house in the city. Those who refused were run off the market, their goods seized. Just a coincidence, of course.

He found out Africville was more than the dump; it was more than its poverty. Found out how for centuries, Halifax raped and robbed Africville and then blamed it for bleeding.

There was a lot of anger in the disposed community of Africville in the years after its destruction. Guilt, too. People felt they'd betrayed Africville, that they'd sold it out. Given up. Abandoned it.

In Africville, there was just Eddie, trying to get himself straight. He'd leave, find more trouble, hurt more people, then limp back home.

Africville always called to him. He felt like a traitor when he wasn't in Africville, like a soldier abandoning his post. He slept uneasily in the city. Even in the dead of winter, he slept better on the frozen fields of Africville than in the warmth of his rented housing in town.

He stopped Africvillians in the street and knocked on doors. He went to taverns and preached Africville. He had a vision of channelling that anger into action, like the Black civil rights movement in the States. He saw a tent city in Africville, hundreds or thousands of people saying, "This is our home" and "We shall overcome." He saw history reversed, houses sprouting out of the land, Africville reborn.

Who would be next? He saw the other local Black communities – Hammonds Plains, Preston, Beechville, Guysborough – banding together to stand together against City encroachments. Africville could do the same, even now.

"Africville was just the tip of the iceberg. Look at Birchtown, Shelburne, Tracadie, Amherst, Sydney. Anywhere there was a large community of Black people, there was Crown land given to them. There was a time when Black people were prosperous. Over the decades, that land was taken," he preached. "We were burnt out, chased off or had to leave on account of conditions. If you look at Africville, that's the same thing they did to us, only it was done in a very fast span of time. Where there was Black people, Black housing, Black industry, you look today and they're gone."

People would shrug uncomfortably.

"What we had, we gave it up for nothing," Eddie would continue. "It was a home for a home, a private deal for a good education for your kid. Petty, pat-on-the-head stuff. Lies."

People didn't want to hear Eddie's rants. People were rebuilding, moving on. Nothing was happening in Africville. Africville got burnt to ashes and nobody was picking up the sticks to fight back.

"Africville wasn't a slum. It wasn't poor. They made it poor," he said. "They promised us so much, promised so much, they gave us so little. We gave up our home for a bunch of words. They deprived us of our wealth, our natural self."

"Man, we ain't gonna get nothing out of it," a former neighbour told him in a dark tavern one day. "The City done what they wanted to do. There's no sense beating your head up against the wall. Get over it, Eddie, and thank God that we got what we got."

The meekness rankled Eddie. The attitude that the City didn't do nothing wrong. He took a drink.

"The City didn't rescue us from poverty – they created that misery!" he shouted.

"Man, we lived off the dump," the man said.

"They threw the dump on us! Just like they did with the prison, the abattoir and the disease hospital. We did what we had to do to survive," he yelled, well worked up. "I carried food off the dump so my sisters and brothers could eat!"

The man just shook his head.

"You're wasting your time. We're not going to get nothing out of it. Forget it. Get on with your life and enjoy what we got," he said, turning back to his beer.

Eddie glared. Eddie was shaking with anger. He wasn't ready to forget. He tried; the booze just made him insane.

The only sane thing he knew how to do was be in Africville.

The man took a drink, stared at the wall.

Eddie walked back to Africville. He'd fish and swim in the day, build little structures and tear them down. The dump was still there, still providing the necessities of life.

35

The dump grew, the waters lapped against the shore, but the people were gone. The prison and hospital had been taken down, too. On the outlines of the streets, a few houses still stood around the turn. It was now a ghost town and the City went about burying the ghosts.

The "blight of Halifax" was gone. Time to demolish the memory. Forget it. Move on. Nothing to see here.

Eddie stayed, watching the final deletion of his world.

Buried Africville seeped through the earth and into Eddie's damaged veins. His roots grew into the soil. The bones of his ancestors called to him from deep below. Eddie healed. The booze left his system. His mind cleared.

In the fall of 1970, Terry, a friend from Saskatoon, gave him a truck with a little house on the back. Terry was a university student and a very special man. It wasn't just the big Jesus beard and long hair: Eddie was pretty sure Terry was working directly for God. Terry was so bright and clear and strong that Eddie felt shy. He was embarrassed and his conviction of Terry's divine nature made him feel a little cuckoo. Terry didn't seem to mind. He and his friends visited Eddie, making sure he had food and wasn't using drugs. For a while, Eddie was sure someone was pranking him into believing Terry was divine. Then again, he'd think, Jesus once walked around just like an ordinary man. He made people feel cuckoo, too.

Eddie took the truck house and set it up down by Tibby's Pond. The protest had its first building. His dream of a resurrected Africville had its first home.

For a while, he had a job at the George Dixon Centre. Fitting – one

Africville fighter earning his living in the recreation centre named for another. Little Chocolate lived on.

The longer Eddie stayed in Africville, the more sane he felt. The paranoia faded. He knew where he was. He knew who he was.

The cops stopped by regularly, telling him to move on, but they kept to a mild level of harassment. Eddie lectured them on Africville, told them whose land they were trespassing on and invited them to go arrest themselves.

He had another visitor, though he never saw her. Stephanie Sparks was living in Halifax then, but when her mom stepped out on the weekends and home life was bad, Stephanie would run away to Africville. She stopped in the woods above the plains leading to the Basin and built a tent out of two abandoned car seats.

She watched Eddie through the tall grass. He'd sit around playing cards with friends, go fishing, gut and dry the fish, or just wander around the ruins of Africville. He'd strum a guitar. Dig mussels. Cook. Some houses were still piles of timber then, with furniture and clothing clinging to the broken skeletons. It was like the dump had taken over Africville.

Eddie was highly strung. The police stayed far back. He was like a roadside bomb with a faulty trigger. Stephanie stayed well back, too.

Until he went into town.

When she saw Eddie leave for town on his bicycle, she'd sneak into his truck and steal a bit of food. She took some soap, once, and tried to clean herself in the Basin, but the Ivory soap turned into a solid on her skin with the salt water and she couldn't wash it off. She had to walk carefully, or she'd trip over the foundations covered by the long grass.

When Eddie got back, she was safely in the tent in the woods again. She would watch him discover the missing food and scratch his perplexed head, but he never saw Stephanie.

Back then, she was certain he'd win – he'd get his land back.

One day a few years into the protest, Eddie's little truck house vanished when he left Africville for a few days. He found it in the dump, broken up and tipped over into the trash heap. Someone told him the City had done it.

He asked the City.

It shrugged.

Eddie got a tent and returned to the protest site.

36

"Nigger! Get out of here, Blackie!" a man screamed late at night from the road above Africville. The new bridge was operating, its ramps running over Pa Carvery's land, and cars whizzed passed around the clock. Sometimes they stopped and the drivers shouted abuse down at Eddie. "Go back to Africa!"

Sometimes they'd come down to his tent in groups of six or eight, throwing rocks, firing pellet guns and taunting him with death threats. Sometimes they'd come out just for that occasion, but other times they just happened to be passing by. Police would turn up and likewise urge Eddie to get lost.

Eddie awoke to gunshots. His mind flashed back to the cops shooting his dog, but the cold told him he wasn't in the Africville of his childhood.

"Get out of here!" a voice shouted. Another shot.

"You couldn't hit the broad side of a barn, you son of a bitch!" screamed Eddie, looking for a weapon. He found an axe. He burst out of his tent and started running, stark naked, in zig zags so they couldn't shoot him. The attackers slammed the car doors shut and squealed off before Crazy Eddie could reach them.

Eddie had other visitors, too – friendly ones. People from Australia, China and Europe, drawn by the recluse in the park. He told them about Africville.

It was long days, longer nights. The summer was pleasant, the winter deadly.

Someone burned his tent down while he was in the city. Eddie got another.

37

Drifting comfortlessly from woman to woman, he got a white girl pregnant. Her family opposed her relationship with a Black man and sent her to Montreal to visit Dr. Henry Morgentaler's new abortion clinic. Eddie knew nothing about it. He called her house after not hearing from her for a few days.

Her grandmother answered and laughed at him when he asked to speak with her granddaughter.

"It's over. You'll never see her again and you'll never see that baby," she gloated. "We sent her to Montreal. You'll never find her. She's going to get an abortion and you're not going to have that baby."

Eddie hung up, shocked. He left Uniacke Square and started walking. He walked and cried and prayed for his girl and their unborn baby, criss-crossing the town. He was in love with the girl and in love with their unborn child. He went to Montreal.

He walked from one end of the city to the other, crossing and recrossing the town at every angle for days. Two weeks later, he hit the end of the island of Montreal, walking the last block until he ran into the water. He hadn't seen any sign of his girl. He turned down a sidestreet back into town, wiping tears away.

The girl stood in front of him, staring wide-eyed.

He shouted her name, too amazed to believe it.

"Eddie," she said, softly. A sadness had flooded her face since Eddie had seen her last. She looked troubled, sleepless. He imagined he looked even worse. Her eyes flitted up to the sign over the door she was about to enter.

Morgentaler's clinic.

"Eddie," she repeated. "My family. They're making me do this."

Eddie covered the remaining distance between them and pulled her in for a hug, their tiny baby in her belly between them.

"Please, please don't do it!" Eddie begged. "Come back to Halifax and have the baby. I'll raise it – you'll be free of it. Please, don't kill our baby."

She stopped her gulping tears, pulled herself together.

"Okay. Okay, Eddie. I'll have the baby," she whispered.

Eddie hugged her like a drowning man clinging to a rock. He walked her to her accommodations and they promised to meet up in Halifax.

They did. She gave birth to a son: Eddie Leo Carvery the Second. The baby came home and Eddie raised him with the help of his mother and Irvine.

38

Eddie spent most of the early 1970s at the Seaway Tavern. He and his friends would meet there in the morning and get drunk. Victor was there, too. One friend, Jimmy, ran a tattoo shop, so he was making some money. They eventually moved their drinking to the tattoo shop, which quickly became the centre of Eddie's world.

Jimmy was a few years older than Eddie. He was smart, and a talented tattoo artist.

"You know, you're white, Jimmy, but you're like a brother. You're just one of the boys," Eddie told him one day.

Jimmy just laughed.

The two men had a lot in common, not least their mutual love for booze. Jimmy's tattoo shop was a great place to shoot the shit, drink the shit and watch the world go by. Sailors would come in with tall tales, get a tattoo and head back to sea. The money they left behind was enough to keep the gang in booze for another day or two.

Eddie still worked at the George Dixon Centre. He'd been there for a year, logged his sensitivity training and was in line to work on a million-dollar project involving youth hostels. He was going to be a community organizer. Eddie felt great – he was working with smart people who cared about his opinion and heading for better things. In 1970, he started attending the new Transition Year Program (TYP), a one-year course designed to help Black and Mi'kmaq students who weren't ready for post-secondary education prepare to study at Dalhousie University. Irvine joined the same year as Eddie. Eddie met a nice woman. Got married.

Then, he followed two friends to a house on Argyle Street. They met a man called Sam. Sam introduced Eddie to his new best friend: speed.

Sam sat there with a syringe, explaining how the new drug worked.

"I'll poke it in you, you'll get a rush, and you'll feel like a million dollars," Sam said. Sam, Eddie found out later, was an ex-cop.

Eddie looked at his two friends, who were getting ready for a hit themselves. He shrugged, rolled up his sleeve, and extended his arm. Sam prepared the syringe, found a vein, plugged it in and –

Eddie's life changed forever.

The drug hit his veins and sprinted through his body, blazing up the blood like a wildfire; Eddie could smell his brains burning. In seconds, he jetted from a shabby house in Halifax to Utopia. All of his worries and insecurities fell away as he blasted through the roof.

He collapsed, grinning, crying, rambling.

Ten hours later, Eddie was still wide awake, still grinning, still sprinting around the city. He felt immortal, supersmart and ready to change the world.

Who needed to know about the speed?

Who could tell?

Everybody could tell.

Eddie was a junkie-in-training.

"I feel like Adam and Eve," he mumbled to himself. He'd committed the ultimate sin and prayed God wouldn't find out. But always, he heard footsteps in the garden in the cool of the day.

Eddie ran.

His interest in the TYP program faded. Work seemed pointless. He couldn't even find his place of work half the time, his brain was so burnt. His marriage was shaking like a cheap house on an earthquake fault line.

His wife was pregnant.

Eddie was excited about that, when he wasn't stoned.

Eddie got a call from a friend in Montreal. Jane needed help. Money. Eddie sent it to her. She came home.

"Thanks, Eddie," she told him one night.

"No problem," he said, thoughts of his wife vanishing like ice in fire.

"I want to reward you," Jane said.

"Well, how're you going to do that?"

Jane smiled.

"Don't worry, I can't get pregnant," she said, moving in. "I just want to sleep with you one time. No one will ever know."

Eddie caved like a cardboard wall.

They spent the night together.

Turns out Jane could get pregnant.

Eddie was a father-to-be again, and an ex-husband-to-be. His wife dumped him hard, and his world went boom.

He was struggling at school.

Work wasn't working.

People scowled at him.

The speed was still there, though. It still loved Eddie. He took another hit from his faithful mistress.

Three days later, Eddie was still wide awake, still grinning, still sprinting around the city, looking for a hit. He found his workmate and demanded he tell him where he could find another hit.

"Try Tom," he said, pulling Eddie's hands off his shirt.

He pointed Eddie to the South End.

Tom sold him it by the spoonful, $25 for five hits. Enough for three days.

One hit, and all his problems went away. Speed took its liberating course through his veins and he was responsible for nothing but enjoying euphoria.

Soon, Eddie was doing four or five spoons a day. It was an expensive habit. Eddie dropped out of TYP and work, and started working for Tom.

What else could he do? He could barely walk down the street anymore. He had forgotten how to read and write. He could barely talk.

All he could do was speed.

Tom needed a bodyguard of sorts, a man who could both menace and act as a cushion between the debtor and Tom's real heavies. Eddie would protect Tom when he did deliveries and convince people to pay up when they were late. He'd take road trips to Montreal to bring in more speed. In exchange, Tom kept him stoned.

Eddie lived in a fog with no past, no future, just present. He was a dog on a leash, a slave in the field, a shield in front of Tom. Tom used him as a sharp stick to poke people.

Tom kept him stoned.

Crazy Eddie kept Tom safe.

Eddie hardly slept, ate or drank. He'd be awake for twenty-three days a month, wandering the city twenty-four hours a day. He had a network of places to crash when he needed to. He stayed away from Uniacke Square as much as he could. His mother didn't need to see this.

He went to Daisy's home when he was really bad. Irvine was still there. He was finishing TYP and starting his working life. Eddie's younger brother shook his head in mute anger as his older brother crashed into his world once again, sending everything flying.

How did Eddie earn his drugs when he was thus incapacitated at home? Eddie had a neighbour and friend called Mike. Mike lived across the Square. Mike was also a speed junkie. Mike had a problem, though. He only had one arm, so he couldn't inject the drugs to get himself high. Eddie helped and Mike shared his drugs, so Eddie could stay stoned.

39

When the drugs got hold of Eddie, it was like having a wild animal in the house. A dangerous beast with sharp claws and more strength than he realized. Irvine tried to limit the damage his older brother did to the home.

Irvine watched Eddie's marriage blow up, watched his big brother stumble deeper into drugs. Eddie and Jane moved into Daisy's house.

"Them guys are crazy," Irvine muttered to himself as Eddie staggered out the door in search of another hit.

"Can I borrow your car?" Eddie asked him one day. He was sober and it seemed he might be able to operate a motor vehicle, so Irvine lent it to him. "Just for a few hours," Irvine said as Eddie ran out the door holding the car keys.

Irvine didn't see his car again for four days.

"I'm not lending it to you any more," he complained when Eddie finally brought it back.

Eddie was crazy. Eddie was violent. Eddie was awake. All the time.

The drugs came first, always, without question. Before family, before friends, before decency, before dogs. Eddie always had dogs but in those days, he couldn't even keep himself clean, let alone the dogs. So Irvine would clean up after the dogs, clean up after Eddie, make sure Eddie didn't come home too crazy. Daisy was still there, as was Eddie's son and their sister Priscilla.

Daisy wouldn't put Eddie out, though she hated it when he was stoned at home. She'd give him money and support him anyway she could. Irvine looked after Daisy and Eddie and Eddie's children and Eddie's everything else.

40

Eddie didn't spend so much time at the tattoo shop, though he kept in touch with Jimmy. Staying high was a full-time occupation. He called Jimmy to borrow his car to do a job for Tom. Jimmy said no problem, here are the keys. Eddie smashed it up and brought it home, calling Jimmy to apologize. Jimmy said it was cool and came over late one night to get the car and join Eddie for a job in Fairview. Eddie was sitting in the basement of Daisy's house, putting his guns in order. Two were laid out on the bed and he had a .22 in his hands. The cartridge was stuck, and he was trying to pry it loose.

"You look awful," Jimmy said as he came in. "You look sick."

Eddie looked up at him, didn't say anything.

Jimmy sat down.

"You need to knock it loose," Jimmy explained, watching a fogged-out Eddie struggle with the .22.

"I got it," Eddie mumbled, yanking on the cartridge. It wouldn't budge.

"Let me try," Jimmy said, reaching for the gun.

"I got it!" Eddie said, trying to keep his voice down. Irvine and Daisy were upstairs, probably asleep, given the hour.

"Give it to me," Jimmy repeated, grabbing the gun from Eddie. "You'll never get it like that. You gotta hit the – "

The gun went off when Jimmy smacked it.

Eddie and Jimmy looked at each other. Jimmy slumped to the floor, smoke drifting out of a hole in his chest.

Eddie stared in shock.

The cops came. Eddie's soul was in the twilight zone, but they sent his body to the hospital. Doctors and nurses tried to get blood out of his damaged veins and it came out like brown snot mixed with little globs of red. After he was stable, he went to jail. He stood trial for Jimmy's death, but the court blamed the faulty gun and sent a numbed-out Eddie stumbling back to the street, an innocent man stained in permanent blood.

41

"You always have another interest that comes before the responsibilities of your relationships," Irvine lectured Eddie of his love affair with booze and speed. Since Jimmy's death, Eddie had barely surfaced for air. "You always put that first. You expect any partner to understand it completely and to follow you. If they don't, you say they don't understand you, they don't love you."

Eddie didn't hear it.

He was locked in a silent prison, an insane asylum for one. He worked for Tom long enough to get another hit, pick the scabs off his arms and plunge the needle in. He sank beneath the streets, walking in a world of subterranean fear and paranoia. He heard that the speed was a government experiment. That people were curious how it would affect people and he was a guinea pig.

He'd get arrested, tell the cops that he wasn't Eddie Carvery, that Eddie Carvery was his brother, and they'd let him go like it was a good joke. So many Carverys.

He watched a young woman try her first hit and die on the spot.

Eddie pissed somebody off and they tried to kill him with a hot fix. It looked like speed, but it was horse tranquilizers. Enough to kill three men, but not Eddie. Almost. The world faded to a single point of black. He was in his mother's house and he didn't want to die in his mother's house. He fought hard, pulled himself back from oblivion.

"Eddie, go to the hospital," his mother pleaded with him. She prayed for her son.

He hated hospitals. He was terrified he was going to get locked up for good in a padded room.

He was sure every shot was his last. If he injected any more speed, it'd kill him. Half the time, he couldn't even find a vein. The blood tunnels would turn sideways and spit the needle out across the room.

His hands shook all the time. He didn't sleep. Speed doth murder sleep, killing the death of each day's life, turning men into ghouls beyond the reach of even the grave's slumber.

Eddie was amazed he could sit down and hold a conversation with his mother. He certainly couldn't hold a pen. He'd tried. It kept dropping to the floor. He couldn't get the grip right.

Every time he tried something, he failed. TYP: fail. Marriage: fail. Work: fail. When he failed, when there was no solution, no hope, there was always violence. Eddie was good at violence. He could succeed at violence. He knew how to grab a man's respect by grabbing his throat. He knew how to make himself taller by knocking another man down. Women, too. Eddie didn't get far into a relationship before he tried to dominate it with punches, kicks and bites.

Daisy told him to go back to Africville, to carry on her protest.

"It would be good therapy for you, Eddie. You could get strong in Africville. Heal," she said when he was sober enough to listen. "The only way to do this is you protest by walking the walk. Don't talk it – do it."

Eddie, his mind on his next hit, nodded.

42

Eddie met Dawn in 1976. Dawn recognized him – she used to babysit for him and his first wife. He didn't remember her. It was a while ago, and she'd changed. They clicked from the start, like magic, Eddie said. In the middle of their encounter, Eddie jerked away.

"You bleeding?" he asked, voice shaking. In the dim light, it looked like Dawn was covered in blood.

"No," she said, panic lighting her eyes. Eddie was covered in blood.

"Are you menstruating?" Eddie asked.

"No!" she said, scared.

Blood was everywhere. It soaked the bed, and their hair and clothes were dripping crimson. They ran into the bathroom and filled the tub. In they jumped, turning the water red as tomato juice.

When they drained the tub, there wasn't a cut between them.

So what was all that blood? So much that if you strung up ten men and bled them to death, you wouldn't get that much blood.

Eddie took it as a spiritual blood-spilling, a visionary expression of God's condemnation of his activities. He could rinse himself clean, but the blood would never come off now, not with all the waters of the Atlantic.

Whatever it was, it winched Dawn and Eddie closer together and he brought her home to meet his mother and move in with him.

That meant Jane had to go, so he kicked her out, blaming her in the process. He was awful to her anyway, so maybe that was a lucky break for her.

43

By the late 1970s, Eddie was unemployed, strung out and stressed. To ratchet up the tension, Dawn gave birth to another baby, another mouth to feed, another set of lungs to scream.

After a violent, wall-shaking confrontation, she stormed out, taking the baby. Eddie had run around on her. He shouted at her that it was her fault.

He swirled deeper into himself. Booze wasn't enough and pot only took the edge off, so he turned to his ever-faithful mistress: speed. She always believed in him, always made him feel fantastic. His mind disintegrated and the remaining rump of paranoid insanity took over his life.

His life imploded. Everything that was normal became abnormal. Sleepless, paranoid, strung out and desperate for a fix, Eddie waved goodbye to Eddie and became a full-time junkie, a speed freak, another piece of trash blowing around the streets of Halifax.

Eddie convinced himself that by plugging his arms full of drugs and his brains full of booze, he was keeping it from going into the arms and brains of other Africvillians.

What a hero!

His battered brain crashed about his skull, turning the world upside down and sideways. He got more guns to protect himself.

One day he thought, that's enough, as his wife and life faded further from view. He gobbled handfuls of pills, spilling them onto the floor, picking them up and chucking them back. The pain dulled to agony.

The world came into focus.

A bleak landscape. A ruined world with no future and a buried past.

He washed the pills down with bottles.

He fell into a blackness.

44

Eddie woke up weeks later. Machines beeped around him in an unbearably light room. Nurses and doctors announced he was a goner, a coma victim forever, human meat slowly turning into vegetable.

His friend George stood beside him.

His mother came in.

His father.

George told Daisy how Eddie had called him in desperation, mumbling about pointlessness and pills. George had hopped in his taxi and sped to Eddie's house, pulled the unconscious junkie into his car and took him to the hospital.

Doctors pumped out his stomach.

Eddie tried to speak, but no sound. Tried to move. Nothing.

Everyone left.

Eddie was alone in a bright, beeping room. His hands woke up, and his feet. Legs and arms, too. Eddie rolled off the bed and crashed on the linoleum floor, tubes and wires ripping out of his body. Machines beeped angrily.

He staggered to the closet. Wrapped his clothes around him and stumbled into the hall. Fell down the stairs. Tumbled out the door and crawled to the nearest house he knew.

His old friend smiled and handed him a syringe.

Eddie jammed it into his arm.

The old euphoria pumped back in.

He sighed.

Lay down.

Rested.

Utopia.

Later, he staggered home. His mother screamed at the ghastly arrival of her ghostly son. Eddie pulled himself up to his room and fell into a shorter coma.

45

Eddie sped to speed houses to speed speed into his veins. Sped to speed jobs to rob people, rumble people, scare people to get money to get speed.

And booze.

Why not get some?

Everyone else was out to get him.

Sped up, he went to the tavern.

Jimmy was dead two years, so Eddie sped alone.

Jimmy's blood washed out of the world soon enough, but it still soaked Eddie's addled mind. He'd close his eyes and there would be Jimmy, rising with smoke puffing out of a hole in his chest.

Eddie drank and sped.

Eddie was a human dump, a walking infectious diseases hospital, a bone prison for one.

Eddie spent the day drinking in the pub.

"Hey Eddie, want to go rabbit hunting?" a friend asked.

Eddie looked at him.

"It's nighttime."

Some brain functions were still working.

"Tomorrow, Eddie. Tomorrow," the friend assured him.

Eddie thought. Shrugged. "Don't have a gun for hunting."

"No problem. I have a .22 you can borrow. Hang on," he said, leaving the bar.

He returned and handed Eddie the rifle.

"I'll get you in the morning," the friend said, departing.

Eddie went home.

His muddled brain was in a bad mood, worsened by the crying of his baby daughter. Eddie was ranting and raving, hollering in a drunken rage. He fought with his wife, grabbed the rifle and threw himself on the bed in a fury. He grabbed the gun, loaded it, unloaded it, loaded it, unloaded it, loaded –

The gun went off, blasting a bullet into the steel bunk, ricocheting to the ceiling, hitting the light fixture and bouncing straight down into his baby daughter.

Eddie's world died. He blacked out. It was winter and the room was blue. Next time he came round, it was summer and the room was brown.

46

The Africville Genealogy Society was formed in 1982, twelve years into Eddie's protest. The Africville diaspora was getting on with their new lives in Halifax and beyond, but the memory of Africville was starting to fade. For white people, "Africville" meant the shanty town squatters who lived in shacks at the dump and who had been mercifully relocated, though perhaps the City could have done it more sensitively. A lot of Black people felt the same way. "Africville" meant a blight, a shameful memory best forgotten. Genealogy was formed to revive the old memories of Africville – the village and the people who lived proudly by Bedford Basin, the people who had the dump dumped on them.

Eddie's cousin Deborah Dickson started Genealogy with her childhood best friends, Brenda Steed and Linda Mantley. Brenda was the daughter of Leon Steed. People hadn't forgotten Africville – families still went "home" all through the 1970s and 1980s. All you'd have to do was make a call, then they'd make a call, and next thing you knew you'd have a big summer picnic out on the shores of Bedford Basin.

It wasn't enough.

"It got so we'd never see anyone from out home unless it was at Christmastime or Easter, or if we happened to run into them at a funeral or a wedding," Brenda explained. "The ones who were children at the time of the relocation grew up and began having children of their own and we didn't even recognize them on the street. We felt like we were losing our identity."

They formed Genealogy to stop that. Eddie was spending more time at his Africville camp in those days, grieving for his lost daughter, trying to hold onto his sanity, trying to stay away from the drugs. His father had collapsed after his son Raymond was killed by that truck and Eddie spiralled down the same fissures of Hell when his baby girl was killed.

Debbie asked Eddie to join Genealogy. He asked her to join the protest. She declined. He declined.

Genealogy organized a reunion in the summer of 1982, an "Acquaintance Day." Dozens of displaced Africvillians and their descendents came home to pitch chairs on the dirt fields by the blue shore, sitting side by side, just like in the old days. It wasn't just a chance to see old faces, but to keep the soul of Africville alive – its traditions. Respect your elders. Honour your women. Fight for what's yours.

Eddie was happy for the company and to see old friends, but he wanted them to stay. He begged his old neighbours not to go back to their homes and lives, but to join the protest.

People got angry with him. People felt bad that they had left Africville. People wore the guilt for what the City had done.

"We do have an argument. We should stay," Eddie pleaded.

People looked at him. With sympathy, pity and disdain.

And told him he was crazy.

"It's over, Eddie. You need to move on."

Some had done well, some had done badly and no one wanted to talk about it. Eddie saw the fear that they'd sold out Africville, that they'd betrayed their home, rotting in their guts.

After the summer reunion, Eddie was alone again. Lots of people offered him a place to stay. He had a place to stay. He stayed. He thought about what people had said about him. He thought about how he used to be, and still was sometimes. But he knew he had worth. He knew he could be fixed.

That long fall, he countered the loneliness with prayer. He thought about fairness, about conviction, about how hard he was willing to fight. He thought about his mother and grandmother. No matter how dark the night, light came with the morning. Another winter settled over the ghosts of Africville.

The next summer, Genealogy turned the get-together into a sleepover. Whole families returned to Africville from all over Halifax – and all over the world. They pitched a tent or parked a trailer where their old home once stood, so that for a few days, Africville was reborn.

Then, they left, gone for another year.

47

In 1984, Eddie, Victor and Irvine held an Africville summit of their own. They told the old stories, talked about how the memory Africville was falling under the water, slipping away, losing its good name. How Genealogy was reclaiming the name. Should they join?

"Something has to be done," the brothers agreed, and that was the last thing they'd agree on for a very long time.

They wrote up a presentation. They took it to City Council and told them what had to be done about Africville. City Council listened politely and filed their presentation in the dank basements of City Hall.

"You know, guys, we need to become a part of the society," Irvine said to his brothers. "That needs to be our vehicle, our voice."

Irvine saw the solution coming from the inside and that they needed to work from the inside to make it happen.

Eddie and Victor shook their heads. They preferred to be on the outside, unconstrained by the cumbersomeness of a large organization. Inside, it was too risky that you'd get paid, forget who you were and abandon Africville all over again.

"It'll only get in the way," Victor protested of Genealogy. "I don't want to be a part of it."

"That's fine. That's your choice, but I think that this is the way to go," Irvine argued.

"It's gotta be like this," Eddie said, meaning the hard, lonely protest.

"Eddie, the real world doesn't work like that. You have to be able to negotiate, you have to be able to reach compromise. If you go up against a power structure and they say no to you and they have all the power, then you can be as right as rain – it ain't going to make a difference. You're not going to get anywhere. You have to be able to find a middle road. You have to be able to find their Achilles' heel and attack the Achilles' heel. Then you can make some difference," Irvine said. "In doing that, you have to bring the people along. You have to get some consensus as to what the people want."

The story of Africville wasn't being told, he said. Even people from Africville were forgetting. Their children didn't know the stories. The only thing they knew was the worst pictures of the worst parts of town, taken by the newspapers as Africville convulsed in its death throes.

"We need to tell the story of Africville through the eyes of the people of Africville," Irvine argued. "People have got to hear our story from our perspective."

Irvine joined the Africville Genealogy Society. Eddie and Victor stayed outside.

Daisy Carvery's three sons broke off onto two paths, all looking for a way home.

48

Irvine Carvery was soon elected president of the Africville Genealogy Society. In 1989, Genealogy organized a major exhibit at Mount Saint Vincent University, located just across the Basin from Africville. It gathered stories, linens, fine china, old photos, even a pulpit someone had rescued from the church, to show Halifax the lie it had been telling itself about Africville. This was no slum.

It was hard work, rescuing the stories of Africville. Irvine met with older folks. At first, they wouldn't even talk about Africville – shame clung to memories like mould. That, and fatigue. Irvine wasn't the first to ask them to share their stories. University students, professors, human rights activists, researchers, reporters – they all trooped through Africville, and through the Africville diaspora, took their stories, and never came back.

"I don't want to talk about it no more. It's finished," an elder said.

Irvine heard him out. Got his story. Got it back to him.

The exhibit opened with a potent service at the Cornwallis Street Baptist Church in October 1989. Cornwallis Street was the mother church to the Africville diaspora. The celebrated pastor of East Preston Baptist Church, Donald Skeir, gave the sermon.

"The leaders of our land can go all across this world talking about human rights, but let us never forget the Black people in a community called Africville," he told the packed church. "They too were oppressed and depressed. But they have survived because they have that spirit within them that has motivated our people for three hundred years." The church burst into Amens and loud applause.

In November 1989, some of the key players in the destruction of Africville gathered to speak to some of the people they had evicted from their homeland. Allan O'Brien, mayor of Halifax from 1966 to 1970, was there. Eddie's older brother Dickie was there. Irvine was there. Everyone was there.

The National Film Board of Canada was there. It made a movie: *Remember Africville*. It opens with footage from a 1970s interview with Irvine, who's sporting a big beard, bushy hair and a groovy hat. He's standing in Uniacke Square. A reporter asks him where he's from.

"I'm from Africville," he says. It cuts to an emotional, much older Leon Steed, moved to tears as he describes his destroyed village.

At the public meeting in 1989, the Halifax mayor who carried out the destruction of Africville said other people had made him do it.

"We accepted the advice of City staff, the advice of an outside expert, and the advice of the Human Rights Advisory Committee," O'Brien said, reading from a piece of paper. "Second, we, the members of the council, chose relocation over all other alternatives."

Alternatives? There were alternatives?

"When I first arrived in Halifax in 1957, I walked along Barrington Street and I saw no coloured people. In those days, we were coloured. We were not yet Black," Gus Wedderburn told the meeting. The West Indies man was one of the out-of-towners whom the City had invited to sit on the Halifax Human Rights Advisory Committee, a progressive-sounding group that had provided covering palliative care as Africville took its last breaths.

Sad and thoughtful, Wedderburn continued speaking in a quiet voice. "I said to my friends, 'Where are the coloured people of Halifax?' And they said to me, 'They live in a place called Africville.' And I asked, 'Where is Africville? I would like to see Africville. Would someone take me to Africville?' Where the pavement ended, Africville began. I did not see the flowers," he said, holding up a photo of Africville seen through red flowers.

Wedderburn told the meeting what he did see: exposed concrete pipes carrying sewage from Halifax into Africville's waters. "I saw my brothers scavenging on the dump," he remembered.

Later, after his brief drive through Africville, he read about a family burning old car batteries to stave off the cold. It was Christmas. They wound up in the hospital with lead poisoning.

"I asked myself the question, 'God, what is this? What is this?'" Wedderburn said emotionally as everyone listened in absolute silence. "I did not see the flowers."

Edward Carvery is in the film, too, sticking up for Africville. Dickie fights back tears as he tells about seeing the church demolished at three in the morning.

It catches up with Leon Steed, too.

Do you enjoy talking about Africville? a reporter asks him.

"No, I don't."

Why not?

"Because it hurts me."

Steed turns away, tears rolling down his wrinkled face.

Why does it hurt you?

"Because it's one of the nicest little communities I ever lived in. I've been around this world twice and I never met a place like Africville," he says, looking down, crying.

But Mr. Steed, everybody thought it was such a bad place.

He looks up, steel suddenly in his voice. "Who?"

The people who tore it down.

"Oh, the people who tore it down," he says angrily. "It was not to us. It was a heaven. A home. A real home."

The public meeting, and *Remember Africville*, ends with Ruth Johnson breaking the world's heart. She sings, transforming the public meeting into a choir:

Africville, Africville, no more can I call you home,
Africville, Africville, I want to go home.
I was born on the shores of the Bedford Basin,
Long time ago.
All the families lived there as one, you know,
There was no other place we needed to go.
Africville, Africville, no more can I call you home,
Africville, Africville, I want to go home.
The City of Halifax has taken our land
And turned it into a park.
We love that place where we lived so dear,
Africville was a part of our heart.
Africville, Africville, no more can I call you home,
Africville, Africville, I want to go home.

49

Outside of Africville, things kept falling apart for Eddie. He kept looking for redemption, kept finding booze, drugs and violence. He lost himself and his mind, and was on the brink of losing his second family.

His answer, always, was violence followed by remorse followed by self-hatred.

He spent days, weekends, nights or weeks out in Africville, the Hundingo Man on the land, fishing, drinking, thinking. Brooding on Africville, he'd chew over the injustice again and again, driving what remained of his brain insane. Sometimes he would stay in the city for weeks; sometimes he would stay at the protest site for months. Sometimes city life seemed like the real Eddie, and he'd only go Africville to escape, and sometimes only Africville would seem real and city life an escape.

He started cracking up. Well, his friend started cracking up.

As the 1980s wore on, Eddie slowed down with the speed. He got clean in an unexpected way: they stopped making his drug. Whatever experiment was underway, it was closed up, leaving a bunch of grumpy junkies.

Industrious amateur chemists tried to recreate the speed. "But it was never the same," Eddie lamented, "that marvelous, wonderful … it was all that. If you had the stuff, it was pure and if they were to inject you with it, well then, you would know. Instantly, you wouldn't want to eat for at least two or three days. You wasn't sleeping, that's for sure. You were speeding."

Eddie's first year on speed had been like heaven, a new world full of unrecognized genius. Eddie felt like Albert Einstein, patent clerk, his brilliance not understood by the speed-free masses. There was a young Italian guy who'd come to Canada with his family and he got caught by speed. A nice girl called Mary-Lou got hooked. In the end, fifteen of Eddie's speed crew didn't make it out alive.

Everyone was crazy. Death meant nothing, but people died nonetheless.

Heroin came next. Given his prominence in the speed trade, Eddie was the potential point man for bringing it into Halifax. At first, he was interested. He got an advance supply and stashed it in a friend's house. Then he found the friend and his son wrecked by it and decided it wasn't for him. He saw it was a different drug altogether. People would die for speed, but they'd kill for heroin.

"Try Toronto," he told the Sri Lankan dealer, who caught the bus there, then Vancouver, leaving junkie nests behind him.

So he was loosely in the market for a new drug. He found it: crack cocaine. His friend came by singing its praises as it swept through the community. She promised him it was the best high you could get. Eddie was curious and so he tried it. Why not?

He lit the pipe and inhaled.

He shrugged. It wasn't speed. It didn't do much of anything for him. Still, he kept using.

You don't have to like a drug to get addicted to it. Unoffended by his indifference, crack took over Eddie and made him work full-time to feed it. Eddie stopped eating, starting using his food money for the drug. He found work as a cleaner and used that money to pollute his brain.

As he lit the pipe and inhaled, he hated himself. He was a liar, he stank, his hair and beard were dirty, he was losing teeth, his skin was greasy and his clothes were grotesque rags.

He cursed himself as he sucked in the dirty air.

50

The Devil came to visit Eddie one day. He didn't believe it, because he knew the Devil is a spiritual creature, not a person. Nonetheless, there he was, standing like an ordinary man outside of Eddie's camp.

He was smiling.

"Good day, Eddie."

No horns. No tail. No pitchfork.

Still the Devil.

"You're not real," Eddie told him. "You're just a smarty playing the Devil."

The smarty smiled and walked into Eddie's camper. He picked up a giant, empty bottle of booze and squatted. Holding eyes with Eddie, always smiling, he pushed the enormous bottle up his backside.

Eddie's jaw dropped open.

Smiling, smiling, the Devil slowly pulled the massive glass bottle out. It made a squishy popping noise.

He held it out to Eddie in his hand. It was a small bottle of white rum now.

Smaller than the Devil's hand.

"What's that?" Eddie asked.

"You know what it is. It's really good if you drink it," he said. "Take it, Eddie."

Eddie had been off the drugs and drink for a little while. He was riding through life sober, but still needed training wheels to keep from tipping over.

Eddie leaned over and took the rum.

"What do you want, Eddie?"

"Nothing from you, Devil," he said, spitting, drinking.

The Devil was not offended.

"Anything," he said.

Eddie's mind went where he wanted to be: inside his son's girlfriend. He licked his lips. He had been baiting his son for months, luring him closer so he could have his way with her.

The Devil knew this.

He just wanted to hear Eddie say it.

Eddie took the rum.

Eddie told him what he wanted.

He sipped the Devil's poison and headed in town to meet with his son and his son's girlfriend. He was going to play a very terrible game with them.

The stage was set: a dim drinking house perfect for dancing with the Devil. Eddie poured out the fire water, eyes crawling up and down his son's girlfriend's body. Catching her eyes. She looked away. His son tried to talk about anything but her. Eddie was unmovable.

Eddie put his arm around her, groping.

"Stop it!" his son shouted, pushing his father's hands off his girlfriend. Eddie pushed his son away.

His son picked up a tire jack and smashed Eddie in the side of the face, breaking his jaw.

"Oooo!" he screamed, holding his busted face. "Son! How could you do that to me?"

His son flung the tire jack far away, suddenly panicked to see the old man bleeding. The girl screamed and leapt away.

Eddie, howling, held his head and cursed the Devil.

"It really hurts!" he moaned, holding his cracked jaw.

"Oh! Look what I did to my father!" his son cried, bloodshot eyes looking for a way to stop the bleeding.

Eddie heard a laughing. Deep, belly laughing.

He scanned the room and found the man sitting at the next table, head back as he roared with laughter.

It was him.

The man from his camp.

The Devil.

That's Eddie's story, anyway.

51

After the big rush to redevelop Africville in the 1960s, the land sat mostly unused throughout the 1970s and into the 1980s. The northwestern corner was turned into a billion-dollar container pier and the high land, cutting through Pa Carvery's property, became an on-ramp for the new bridge. But the heart of Africville was mostly left as it was after the expulsion.

That changed in the mid-'80s when the City turned the grave of Africville into a dog dung park. Not just any dog dung park, but an award-winning, million-dollar dog dung park. The City sent heavy machinery back into Africville, this time to truck in tons of soil to pour over the remaining foundations and landmarks. The City manufactured rolling hills, planted trees, put in garbage bins and a toilet in the parking lot. The idea was that the people of Halifax would have a nice place to let their dogs play off leash.

Eddie had to keep shifting his tent out of the way of the big trucks hauling the landfill.

He'd chat with the workers.

"It's all over," the driver said, leaning out of the cab. "One of these days, it's going to be all green and forgotten about."

Eddie shouted up, "There's enough of Africville left for our community. When the City wakes up, we can have dream houses out here. We deserve them!"

There was a competition on to win a Dream Home in a new subdivision not far from Africville. New houses were springing up on the hill overlooking Africville. They were not inhabited by Africvillians.

The man shook his head, went back to work, lights flashing, engine roaring, reverse-warning beeping.

Tibby's Pond was filled in, so you couldn't even tell where there had been water. A fenced-in playground sat on top of Joe Skinner's house. Even the dump was buried.

On June 22, 1985, the City had a ribbon-cutting ceremony to officially open Seaview Memorial Park. Memorial? To whom? To what?

Three years later, a sundial was installed inside the park to clarify matters. It reads, "Seaview Memorial Park. Land deeded 1848 – 1969. Dedicated in loving memory of the first Black settlers and all former residents of the community of Campbell Road, Africville and all members of the Seaview United Baptist Church. First Black settlers William Brown, John Brown, Thomas Brown."

Finally, a cryptic inscription:

> To lose your wealth is much,
> To lose your health is more
> To lose your life is such a loss
> That nothing can restore.

That's all you need to know. Now go walk your dog!

52

Eddie's older brother Dickie had a lot of problems. Life didn't always go well for him. In the 1970s, he was in a bad car accident. He was only thirteen months older than Eddie, but it looked like his time was up.

He was living out in Spryfield and had been drinking one night when he lost control of his truck and hit another car. Dickie was thrown from the vehicle, but his stomach caught on the door frame as he went, ripping him open. The doctors tried to put him back together again.

Daisy took the phone call. "Your son is dead," they told her.

"Eddie, go to the hospital," she told him, fighting panic. "Dickie's been killed."

"What?"

"He's been killed in a car accident," she repeated, trying to stay calm.

Eddie flew to the hospital and found Dickie strapped to machines, but not dead. He was all alone in the room with glugging machines slurping at him. It was like robotic vampires sucking his blood out. Eddie pulled the tubes out of his brother and shouted at him.

"Dickie! Dickie! Wake up! What are you doing?"

Dickie's closed eyes fluttered.

"Dickie, wake up! Mamma says you can't die. You got to wake up!"

Dickie stirred.

His eyes flickered open.

He stared at Eddie with heavy, unhappy eyes.

He survived.

Later, he pulled Eddie aside for a chat about his near-death experience.

"You remember when I was in the hospital?" he said.

"Yeah."

"And you called me back?"

"Yeah."

"Well, don't ever do that again. Don't ever bring me back again," Dickie told Eddie.

Years later, deep into the 1980s, Eddie was there again as his older brother lay dying, but that time he didn't call him back.

Eddie was there when his mother died, too, and his father. He went to both wakes, both funerals. He stood at both coffins.

What does he remember of it?

Nothing.

They've not been dead centuries, but he can't even remember who died first. Blame the drugs? The drink?

That, but also Eddie lost in a vortex of pain beyond winters or summers, beyond time.

Same for the funeral of his sister Evelyn.

Whoosh!

What's that?

There go the 1980s.

53

Eddie became an increasingly violent man. His family bore the brunt of it. He tried to get help to find a path out of his drug-fogged world, but nothing helped.

Things ended badly with Dawn. Eddie's bubbling brain thought it caught her cheating (it didn't). He blamed her for wrecking his first marriage for nothing. He blamed her for the collapsing mess of his life. Eddie set on fire everyone who loved him and blamed them for burning him. Decades of anger simmered under the surface like molten lava deep in Eddie's core.

Eddie blew his top.

"You cheated on me!" he screamed. "You're gonna get what you got coming!"

He punched Dawn, bit her and kicked her. She fell and he kept coming. She screamed and he roared. Reeking of alcohol, he filled the room with dark terror.

After, with Dawn now covered in real blood and whimpering on the floor and Eddie exhausted from beating her, he came back to his mind and saw what he had done. Again.

He called the police and told them to come and arrest him.

They showed up with flashing lights and squawking radios.

Dawn was sitting up by that point, nursing her wounds.

"No," she mumbled through her battered face when she saw the police. "It's okay."

The cops hesitated. Eddie told them to arrest him, so they did. They charged him with assault.

While Dawn recovered in hospital and his case worked its way through the courts, a woman he was seeing scored a motherlode of booze. She left it at Eddie's. A kid in a poisoned candy shop, he started chucking it back by the bottle. He kept feeling sober and kept drinking more, deep into the night and back out into the morning. Friends would stop by, drink, get drunk, pass out or leave.

Eddie kept drinking. The rage he felt for his number one enemy bubbled up and boiled over. The low-life scum was responsible for everything that went wrong, for every person Eddie hurt, for Dawn being broken up in hospital and Eddie facing jail again. The hatred solidified and Eddie decided it was time to end it.

He went to his closet and pulled out his thick army overcoat.

It was one a.m.

He drank the bottles empty.

He went into the basement, where he stored his outboard motor and spare gas. He grabbed the freshly filled five-gallon gas can and climbed upstairs.

He lifted the can above his head and poured gasoline all over himself as he sat on the kitchen floor.

He put a cigarette in his mouth.

Lit it.

The world exploded in a transparent blue-hot flame.

As he blacked out in the dense smoke, a face loomed out of the fire and looked at him sadly.

Eddie lost consciousness.

To his surprise, he woke up the next morning. He stood up. Where his ashes should have been was a bright white circle.

The coat was not singed. The gasoline was gone.

The house wasn't burned down.

Eddie wasn't burned down.

Eddie said a prayer. Eddie thought, My life is not my own. I don't have the authority to end it.

Eddie thought, I need to give the selfishness up. I need to give the violence up. I need to give the drugs and booze up.

When Eddie's case finally made it to sentencing, the judge gave him fifteen months in jail. Eddie asked the judge to give him more.

"I hurt her, I hurt myself and I need to get well," he explained. "I don't want to hurt nobody no more. I'm an animal and I need to be fixed."

The judge upped his sentence to three years. It was about 1990.

Eddie resumed the education he had stopped when he left the Ontario jail. He read about alcoholism and what it does to you, how violence creates violence. He concluded that no matter what someone else did, it didn't give him the right to hurt that person.

Eddie was like Winston Churchill's America: you could always count on him to do the right thing, after he'd tried everything else.

He thought Dawn and the kids would be safer with him out of the picture. Freed from his anchor, she could float back to the surface. It was his first time in a federal penitentiary. Springhill. He wasn't popular there – wife-beaters are low on the prison pecking order, and he got pecked. He kept his head down.

That wasn't the worst. The worst was dealing with his cellmate. Eddie was glad to be in prison, glad to pay his debt to society and show his remorse for what he did, glad to get clean, but did he have to do his time with Eddie? Everyone else got a chance to escape from Eddie, but Eddie had to live with the monster all the time.

Was there a way Eddie could save Eddie?

When he came out, it had half worked. He was clean, but his wife was down deeper cracks of hell than before, and also no longer his wife. Pre-prison, he'd had a home and a couple of trucks. Post-prison, his trucks were gone, too, converted into crack, and they'd lost the house. The kids had vanished into Children's Aid.

So much for protecting his family.

He'd also mostly gotten on top of his alcoholism. That was a revelation – it had never occurred to him before that alcohol was an -ism. It was just a part of life, like hamburgers and pop, and being drunk was just another state of being, like being sleepy or angry.

Out of prison, single, sober and homeless, the Hundingo Man returned to his only forever home: Africville.

54

Eddie wasn't the only displaced Nova Scotian coming home. Stephanie Sparks got divorced and moved back to Halifax from Montreal in 1990. Usually, she'd go see Daisy Carvery, but Daisy had died, so Stephanie went to see Eddie in prison. They talked about a lot of things, including drugs. Eddie was clean by then and Stephanie was trying to get clean. Not long after Eddie got out of prison, she signed herself into a hospital to try to purge the drugs. She had only one visitor. Eddie Carvery.

When she broke the addiction and left the hospital, she and Eddie started dating and soon moved in together. They considered themselves married. They'd been together a while when Stephanie's brother sent his twin girls to stay with her, so she and Eddie adopted them. Stephanie understood the protest like few others and supported Eddie as he tried to maintain two lives: husband and father at home and Hundingo Man in Africville.

"If I can't do anything, I know I can do that," he would say. When she first got home, she was between places so she put everything in storage and went back to Africville to pitch her tent with Eddie. Stephanie brought a woman's touch to the camp, tidying it up, doing laundry, keeping it clean. It was a basic life out there. They caught their own fish, boiled their drinking water, took long walks by the shore. For a while, they tried to rebuild a beach.

"It's like going back in time," she'd joke.

In the city, she'd go to the Africville meetings with Eddie, making coffee while the diaspora talked things out.

She stayed all summer and deep into October, moving to Halifax when it got too cold and it was time for the twins to settle into school. Even then, she came out most days with a hot meal and spent weekends with her husband when she could. After staying with Hattie Carvery in Africville's last years, she'd kept coming out with her brothers for picnics and to dive for mussels and lobsters under the bridge. The fishing stopped when the City decided it was unsafe and fined hungry people until they stopped eating the lobster and mussels.

Winter buried Africville deep under snow, making it harder to get out there to check on Eddie. One dark, frozen day, she made her way out despite the deep chill in the air. Her breath puffed out in white clouds, like steam from the trains that still cut through Africville. She found Eddie's camper in darkness. No fire, no growling generator. Just cold, dark stillness.

She approached the camper cautiously, opened the door and caught her breath. Eddie lay as cold and still as the night. His hair and goatee were frozen solid and he was wrapped in his sleeping bag like a mummy. He was in his snowsuit, but that was also covered in ice. The walls were covered in ice. The cups were full of ice.

Stephanie was scared. How long had he been like that? Should she touch him?

"Eddie!" she screamed into the camper. "Are you sleeping or are you dead?"

She didn't want to touch him, just in case he was dead.

Eddie stirred. Took a few minutes to thaw out enough to speak.

"I'm not frozen yet," he mumbled. "Guess the fuel ran out."

He lit a fire and welcomed his wife home. He got pretty sick soon after and when doctors told him he'd die if he kept sleeping in Africville, he starting spending some nights in the city.

He had his first heart attack in 1994. He was forty-eight years old. He was out in the camper with Stephanie when she noticed a weird look on his face.

"You okay?" she asked.

"Fine."

"You don't look fine."

"It's just gas."

It wasn't gas. Stephanie told Eddie to frig off and called his son to come take his old man to the hospital.

Doctors again told him he was flirting with death in those long Africville winters. He thanked them and went home. To Africville.

55

Victor had a business selling fish to the diaspora of Africville, just like he did for his father when he was a kid. He'd worked for the Coast Guard, but it hadn't worked out. He kept finding racist death threats on his bunk on the open sea. One day another sailor burst into his room with a knife, trying to kill him. Victor defended himself and knocked the guy out. The captain agreed with Victor that he'd had no choice, but said, as captain, he also had no choice: he had to let him go. He got Victor to sign papers that he told him would get him a space on another ship. Victor couldn't read well. He signed.

He left the ship and handed his papers in, expecting a paycheque and reassignment.

"Where am I off to now?" he asked.

The clerk looked surprised.

"That was your resignation form," he told him, laughing.

And so that was the end of Victor's dreams of being the first Black captain in the Coast Guard. He was running low on dreams.

Victor went to Genealogy's Africville reunion in the summer of 1994. He hadn't been before, but had decided to go while in church. He heard a message from the Lord in his heart: Take the boys from the church fishing in Africville. Teach them how to be men, how to honour their mothers, fathers and grandparents. How to respect elders and all races.

He told his pastor about it.

"Yes, Victor, the Lord spoke to you. You should do this," his pastor agreed.

So Victor went to the reunion and got a boys' camp going down by the water, on his grandmother's property near what used to be Tibby's Pond. It was a field now. Eddie was living at the far end of Africville then, splitting his time between the protest and Stephanie, and the boisterous main body of the reunion separated the brothers. The group of nine boys pitched five tents and the little congregation sat down with Victor. He told them Bible stories and discussed what they meant.

"Always put the Lord first and you will prosper," he told them. He told them the important role Canada had in the world as a nation that could rise above racism, if people worked hard enough. He kept his own experiences in check, so as not to discourage them.

"If you're not brought up right, there are three ways a man will end up: in prison, in poverty, or dead," he told them. "If you haven't got your education, you're done for."

The boys swam on the shore where Tibby's Pond once entered the Basin. They cooked, played and learned about Africville's history, about the wealth their ancestors had built farming the land and fishing the waters.

The summer reunion wound up. Victor arranged for the boys to stay on a little longer, so as to appreciate the silence of Africville. Up the hill, tents were packed, sad goodbyes said, and Africville left Africville for another year. Victor and the boys stayed down on Granny Pink's land.

A uniformed white man came hastily over the hill. He announced himself as a park superintendent, still puffing from his exertions.

The nervous boys clustered behind Victor.

"Who are you?" Victor asked the man.

The man provided his name and then gave orders.

"Tear down your tents. The reunion is over. If you're not off the property by four p.m., I'll have you removed," he said, nodding in the direction of the boys.

"Excuse me, I don't understand 'removed,'" said Victor, eying the man. Victor was a tall, thin man and towered over the superintendent. "What do you mean?"

"I'll call the authorities and have you removed if you're not off of this property by four o'clock," the man repeated.

The park was quiet. The boys held their breath. The wind stopped. The waves paused. In the silence, Victor heard the church bell ringing in Africville, the church bell the City had bulldozed in the middle of the night thirty years before.

Victor heard it ringing as clearly as the park warden was yelling.

"Can I borrow your cellphone?" he asked the man.

"What do you want my cellphone for?" the warden asked, suspicious.

"So I can phone the authorities and have you removed. Look around you – if you can see anything that the City bought or paid for, I'll leave."

The warden glared.

"You'd better leave, or you'll be forced out," he warned, heading back out of the park.

"Okay, boys, I got to get you out of here. I'm staying, but you got to get home," Victor told the kids. He called the parents of the church boys and told them the camp was over. For the next few hours, Africville was busy as concerned parents retrieved their children.

"I heard the church bell ring," he told them. "Take the children out of here. I've got a lot of work to do, a lot of praying to do. I don't know what's going on in my life."

By evening, Victor was alone. He had a nice house in the city, with a good wife and a good family. And cats. Time to go home?

Victor realized he was home. It was time to stay home.

That night he slept in Africville for the first time since he was a boy.

56

Later that summer, Victor left the protest site to stay in the city for a bit. He still had a business, still had a family. He still had a lot of things to think through. He was arguing with his wife – about money, work, houses – so he went for a long midnight walk with his dog Prince. They wound up in Africville. Wandering in the shadows of the trees, he wondered if he was doing the right thing, devoting his time and energy to Africville.

Going into the city was dangerous. Just one warm meal in a kitchen, you'd think. Just one night in a warm bed, you'd reason. And then, why not another meal? Another night? And the lonely, cold camp looks less and less real. The will to fight dies.

Victor and Prince stopped at the tree that bears no fruit and lay down in the long grass. This was where Granny Pink brought him all those years before to tell him about the slaughter of the Black people of Africville. He closed his eyes and imagined her there with him, saw the old houses surrounding him, heard the rhythm of Africville. He started digging his hands down into the earth, feeling it in his hands as the cool night fell on him.

He felt something solid in his hands. He felt something nudging his feet. He could hear Prince breathing. Victor opened his eyes and gazed at the starry night. Closed his eyes. Felt another nudge. Started getting scared, thinking rats.

Anther nudge.

He opened his eyes.

Rabbits.

Dozens of rabbits, swarming the hill.

Victor smiled.

It seemed a good omen.

His hands dug in the dirt and he found a stick. He brought it home, left it on the kitchen table as he went to bed.

Over breakfast the next morning, he saw the stick again, only it wasn't. He picked it up and took a good look. It looked like a finger bone.

He went back to the protest.

57

Victor took a walk out to Fairview. He knocked on a door. Eddie opened it. Victor knew about Eddie's protest and had even joined him for a weekend once, but it was different now. He'd heard the church bell ringing. He understood what Eddie's twenty-four-year struggle was all about.

Eddie invited him inside. Eddie was camped out by the shore in Africville, but if he didn't want to see you, you wouldn't see him, and Eddie didn't want to see anyone in those days. Victor didn't know his older brother was still in Africville.

"The Lord spoke to me and I'm out home," Victor announced, sitting at the kitchen table. "I'm in this war and I can't leave. I thought I'd pop over and have a cup of tea."

The brothers talked and agreed to work together. Their cousin Nelson Carvery, son of Pa Carvery, arranged a couple of campers for them and set them up as neighbours inside of Seaview Park, on the land they had grown up on.

Eddie thought about the Old Testament, how the Lord used just one or two people to lead His causes. He thought about David taking on Goliath, about Moses leading his people for forty years, and his brother, Aaron, helping.

Late at night, out in the quiet fields of Africville, the brothers talked.

"You remember the Infectious Diseases Hospital?" Victor asked in the candlelit night, and they'd remember how the once pristine Tibby's Pond had been turned into a frothy-green toxic dump. Victor started to see walls that had imprisoned him from birth. The cell of Rockhead when he was a boy of twelve was nothing compared to the open-air prison the City had made of Africville. Of Africvillians. A prison of poor education, of alienation from the rest of the city, of putting a dump full of toxins in the middle of his home.

"What have you got in your life?" he asked Eddie, talking mostly to himself. "What are you going to leave to be written on your headstone? Nothing! That's a sad way to leave this world, ain't it? You never done nothing for the world and the world never done nothing for you, so when you die, all you got is your name. That's a pauper's grave, by the way. The reason why we can't have nothing on our headstones is because society never gave us a chance to make something out of our lives.

"It's terrible! If the shoe was on the other foot, how would that Caucasian world feel? I'm sure they would've got paid by now. I'm sure they would have their church building built by now. They put me in prison, but the Lord unlocked the gates."

Eddie nodded in the dim light.

58

When winter hit, Eddie and Victor were alone in the park. The dog walkers stopped visiting. Victor's wife came out, asked him to come home. He was home. He wasn't going to leave again.

"When you're called out to fight a fight from Father God himself, then there's nothing in town for me. Absolutely nothing. I have to do what has to be done, and that's to rectify the evil that has been imposed on my community," he told her.

She sighed. Went home.

Victor stayed home.

Eddie had his camper, one made for the back of a truck, up off the ground, raised on train track beams. Victor's was right on the ground, pulling in the permafrost.

Students from Dalhousie University came across Eddie and Victor and learned about the protest. They started coming out with pizza, to eat and talk with the brothers.

In the daytime, Victor and Eddie walked their dogs around Africville. The part of town where Granny Pink had lived, where she kept her post office, and nearby where Eddie and Victor were born, that was all buried under mountains of landfill. But outside of the park, where the grass grew wild, Africville was only lightly buried. Victor started digging up the old foundations, finding bottles and antique remnants of his demolished world. He found an old stroller rotted into the earth, spokes looking like a skeleton. He wondered what child had sat in the stroller back in Africville. He found an old set of steps leading nowhere and put it at the door to the missing church. He started building a shrine of bottles and candles to honour the ghost temple.

Victor rambled up the hill to where a baseball diamond sat next to the old boneland his grandmother had shown him. Along the bridge on-ramp where Uncle Pa Carvery had lived and run his business.

Victor weathered his winter back in Africville, but the isolation was wearing on him. His business was gone and his wife was threatening to divorce him if he didn't come home.

He was home.

He took his life savings and hired a lawyer to dig up the old deeds. He didn't have any more money to start a legal suit to reclaim the land, so he lived on it.

Stephanie dug up old artifacts, too. She and Eddie found old spoons, plates, right down by the water, where people washed their dishes and where people threw broken stuff out. They carted it back to Eddie's camper and stored it. Stephanie took notes every day she was out there, detailing what happened, who came by, when the police knocked on the door, what the weather was like. She stored it in Eddie's camper.

59

In the spring of 1995, the Africville protest was front-page news. Prime Minister Jean Chrétien was coming to Halifax, as was U.S. president Bill Clinton, France's Jacques Chirac, Britain's John Major, Helmut Kohl chancellor of Germany, Lamberto Dini, prime minister of Italy and prime minister Tomiichi Murayama of Japan. From June 15 to June 17, Halifax would host the G7 summit – and the global media that came with it. The City fathers and mothers of Halifax glanced down on Africville and decided having two Black men protesting in a vacant city park would raise too many questions.

The City started sending warnings out to the brothers, urging them to leave.

It began with the park wardens.

"Vic, you and your brother gotta get outta here. They're going to make up a bylaw," a warden warned him.

"This is my grandmother's property and I'm not going to leave it because you say it's a park," Victor said. "Get out of my face. I ain't going nowhere."

The man left, shaking his head.

"You think because we used to have dogs out here, because the police used to come out here and shoot our dogs, that this can be a dog park?" Victor asked his receding form. "That gives them a right to put a dog park here, where we could still be living in our home?"

The media raced back into Africville. "Scandalous!" screamed a headline in the Halifax *Daily News* over a story detailing the City's drive to once again remove the Carverys from Africville. "I don't believe Halifax has a right to call me a squatter on my own land," Eddie told the council as they discussed a bylaw that would fine the brothers $2,000 a day for camping in the park.

"When does this law take effect? When can we expect them to come and take us off to jail? Is it going to be three o'clock in the morning like it was when they tore down our church?" Eddie asked to cheers from the Africville diaspora and their supporters.

He wasn't answered.

The mayor, Walter Fitzgerald, warned the dispossessed Africvillians on hand to stop cheering or he'd throw them out of the chambers. Everyone got five minutes to speak their mind, but Victor didn't take well to being told his time was up.

"Thank you for that one minute, but I'm sure it took you more than five minutes to take Africville," he said to more disobedient cheering.

Lots of people were there to support Eddie and Victor.

One person wasn't. Irvine Carvery, their younger brother. As head of the Africville Genealogy Society, he was fighting to make sure the bylaw didn't put an end to the summer reunion camping.

Eddie and Victor took it as dark personal betrayal. Irvine later said he thought they could have fought the law anyway, using the provisions he got for the summer reunion. Eddie and Victor didn't see it that way.

The City also noted that the church promised three years earlier was on its way. The one Martin Luther King III had broken soil for. It was coming. Any day now.

The media loved the story: brothers split, fighting City Hall and the looming pressure of the G7. Here's a sample of the in-depth reporting: "Brothers Edward and Victor Carvery are squatting in the north-end park because they're jobless and broke, and because they're protesting what happened to their old community," a reporter wrote, citing no one but himself.

Here's his punchy conclusion: "Meanwhile, police are investigating complaints about sex acts in the park. It's a popular meeting place for gay men." He again cited no one but himself. What did this have to do with a decades-old civil rights protest? Who knows?

Another reporter referred to the brothers' "spontaneous" decision to start the protest, as though it was done on a whim. Nobody noticed Eddie's protest was celebrating its twenty-fifth birthday.

As the battle dragged on, the deputy mayor defended the City past and present. "The City of Halifax stands proud and strong that we're a good corporate community, and I don't think the City would treat their people unfairly. I don't think it's ever happened," Pat Pottie opined.

Eddie and Victor and Irvine all agreed: it happened, Mr. Deputy Mayor.

In fact, lots of people agreed on that one. The summit was due to be held in a building called Cornwallis Place – Edward Cornwallis being the English man ordered to found Halifax in 1749. A few years into his rule, he paid white civilians to murder and scalp as many Mi'kmaq children, women and men as they could. Modern Mi'kmaq people didn't think he should be honoured with a building, or all of the streets bearing his name, or the big statue in the South End.

In an August meeting between Africville protesters and the City, Eddie threw that right hook that floored his heckler and earned himself a huge photograph in the local newspaper.

Mayor Fitzgerald got his bylaw to evict Eddie and Victor. Newspapers ran headlines about the battle between the City and the "squatters."

"This is craziness! The anarchy must stop. We just can't allow people to throw us off our own land."

Who said that? Eddie? Victor? Irvine? No. Surely some Africvillian? No. Walter Fitzgerald. The white guy. The mayor.

"Our patience is running out," he added. "We're not going to put up with it much longer."

Irvine got the bylaw loophole protecting the summer reunion. "Eddie and Victor could have used that. I don't know why they didn't just stay there and say, well, read your own bylaw. I'm from Africville and I'm here in the park and I have a right to be here," he later said.

With the new bylaw in hand, the police picked up their campaign to evict the Carvery brothers from Seaview Park.

"You're not allowed to camp a tent in any park in Nova Scotia," an officer told Eddie and Victor. The cops said there was a massive daily fine for disobeying the bylaw: $2,000 a day.

"We ain't going nowhere. Get out of our face and get off of our land until you prove that you bought it," Victor said.

The cops left. Said they'd be back.

Eddie and Victor stayed.

The cops came back.

"You owe the city a lot of money," they said, tallying up the $2,000-a-day fines the brothers had racked up for camping in the park. "If you can't pay it, you're going to wind up in jail."

The brothers stayed.

"Still here?" the cops said, passing by. "You're breaking the ordinances, and you're going to wind up in jail."

"We're not going nowhere," Victor said. "That's the fight. It's a protest. We're not going nowhere, you're not taking nothing, and nothing and nothing. You're going to have to kill us, it's that simple."

The cops shrugged and left.

Deeper into spring, Eddie was wondering why the City didn't just arrest them. Then he thought, maybe they're going to arrest us just before the summit, so that we're in jail when the leaders and media come.

"Okay, it's getting rough," Victor said to Eddie. "Here's what we'll do. One of us is going to get killed, or both of us are going to wind up in jail."

So at three a.m. one May morning in 1995, Eddie and Victor packed up the protest site, moved both trailers out of the park and set them up a few feet on the other side of the new wrought iron fence, on the site of the missing church and the demolished school.

They were outside of the park. They were outside of the bylaw.

"We're happy you boys moved," the officer said the next morning. "It'll make things a lot better. Don't worry, we won't be coming round any more."

Eddie and Victor were satisfied – the whole area was Africville.

"I don't think it was our intention to have a showdown with police because … we have no complaint with the police," Eddie told reporters the next day. "Our complaint is with the City."

"It's a whole new problem," grumbled the mayor.

"They're trespassing. Kick them out," added his deputy, Steve Adams.

Irvine Carvery said Genealogy welcomed his brothers to use the land promised for the church, at least until the church was built. "After that, they're gone. The reason for being there will be gone," he told a reporter.

The mayor was frustrated, but unable to pursue the brothers outside of the fenced-in Seaview Park. "They picked a good place to continue their protest," Walter Fitzgerald conceded.

Eddie and Victor took a day trip to visit family on a farm in East Preston. They had decided to revive another old Africville tradition and keep a few animals on their protest site for food. They selected a big white turkey with a red face. They named it Walter Fitzgerald. The hens, chickens and ducks all took on the names of the City councillors voting to evict the Carverys, except for a duck called Alma. He was named in honour of the Africville Liberation Movement Associates, the title they'd given the protest.

"Let's teach them how to follow us," Victor proposed one day. "Then they can follow us in town and go in City Hall and poop all over the red carpets."

"I'm not sure Alma will be up for it," Eddie warned.

60

Irvine Carvery was facing an unexpected challenge in his fight for the disappeared village of Africville – the City that bulldozed it was about to disappear. The City of Halifax was planning to merge with its neighbours into a supercity.

"We'd better go get some legal advice, because if the old City of Halifax is gone, what responsibility will this new body have for what Halifax did?" Irvine asked the Genealogy society.

He sought a lawyer's opinion. "We don't know the answer to that question, but what we can tell you is that if you file a legal suit against the City of Halifax, under amalgamation that will carry over to the new body," the lawyer said.

So in 1995, Genealogy filed suit against the City of Halifax, seeking reparations for the destruction of Africville. Irvine met with the diaspora to see what they wanted.

"$13 trillion," one man said.

"That's crazy," Irvine said.

Irvine and Genealogy worked out a request. At first, they sought individual compensation – you know, that old house-for-a-house business. But the City promised to fight that all the way to the Supreme Court of Canada. Irvine was up for the fight, but lacking the millions of dollars it would take to carry out the battle.

"Plus, we don't think you can win," the lawyer said. The statute of limitations was up, and you'd have to get that waived, and then you were still in Nova Scotia, whose entire legal system had been declared systemically racist by the 1989 Marshall Inquiry into the 1971 wrongful conviction of a Mi'kmaq man charged with murder.

"You won't win in court," said an African-Nova Scotian judge Irvine knew. "The system is just too stacked against us. Given the history of this province in terms of race relations, you'll never win in court. It would have to go to the Supreme Court."

"We don't have that kind of money. Nothing near it, and no source of money to support it," Irvine said.

So Genealogy agreed to go for a political, not legal, solution. And communal compensation. And that church, please.

61

The G7 rolled into town and hungry reporters quickly found the Africville story. *The New York Times* dispatched a journalist to interview Eddie and Victor in May to learn about their alternative "people's summit."

"The pavement stopped where Africville began, and the tiny waterside community of freed slaves' descendants had neither running water nor streetlights," the story started.

The writer got some of his facts wrong, but painted a rough sketch of the situation. "'We feel our community was stolen from us,' said Eddie Carvery, a jobless sheet-metal worker in Che Guevara military fatigues, standing on the spot where he was born forty-nine years ago. Since last July he and his brother Victor, forty-five, an unemployed house painter, have been living in trailers on the Africville land as a protest. They seek a full-scale public inquiry into the relocation decision, return of some of the land that now lies vacant and eventual compensation for the wrongs they feel were done to the community."

Eddie might have been surprised to learn he was jobless, as he considered the Africville protest full-time work. He might also have been surprised to learn the previous twenty-five years of his protest had been erased. Victor was probably pleased to learn he had grown two years younger.

The New York Times quoted the 1990s City defending the 1960s relocation as progressive: "City officials say the claims have no merit. 'They were taken from living conditions that were not the best, and put in living conditions that were better,' said Deputy Mayor Stephen D. Adams. 'They were given compensation at the time. If they are given more compensation now, then what kind of claim would the native people have from the sale of Manhattan?'"

A talk show radio host agreed it was a raw deal, what happened to Africville, but that was such a long time ago. "How much are we responsible for what happened then?" Besides, don't worry: "The City Council has made a small peace offering. It has proposed to create a $100,000 scholarship fund for Africville descendants and to donate land to rebuild Seaview United Baptist Church, whose original building had been torn down."

Any day now.

62

After the summit, the pressing need to deal with Africville suddenly vanished. The media circus, and the watchful eye of the City, moved on to other things. Eddie and Victor stayed, but the dark winter savaged the brothers. Victor's summer trailer got a hole in it and water trickled down the sides of the camper. A deep freeze gripped the city. Hard winds raced around Bedford Basin and slammed into the tin trailers, freezing the water on the walls. Victor lay in bed, shivering, watching the frost thicken. Everything was glistening white. It was like being back up in the Arctic. Jump, Blackie, jump.

Eddie shivered next door in his camper. They used generators to heat them when they could afford gas. Not tonight. The kerosene heater was out of commission because someone had stolen Victor's kerosene and replaced it with water. He poured the concoction in and it broke the heater.

They had some relief most evenings when a white couple from up the hill came round with a hot meal. "My father was always saying it was wrong," the war veteran said about Africville one night as Victor and Eddie chowed down. "Even the land our house is on belongs to Africville. My father told me the deeds we have are false deeds."

The couple had so far pushed the death grip of winter off the throats of Eddie and Victor.

Not tonight. It was dark, desolate outside. Nobody around for miles. Miles and miles of frozen dead land. Victor roused Eddie and insisted on a midnight walk to get his blood going. They strolled through Africville, braced against the lethal wind knifing in from the choppy water. The trees sparkled in ice. The ground was crunchy snow. Their feet fell through it, leaving holes for footprints.

"We c-c-can't leave," Victor stuttered, breath puffing in white clouds. "It's a w-w-war. This is the f-f-front. We're under the c-c-command of F-f-father God."

Eddie murmured agreement, pulled his collar up over his bearded mouth. They rubbed their arms, shivering through the trees like ghosts, dogs playing at their feet. They kicked the snow to keep from dying. Another wind howled in like a whip. Victor staggered, fell to his knees, breaking boards of snow. Cars roared distantly over Pa Carvery's land and rumbled across the bridge. Africville swam before his eyes. Eddie helped him stagger back to the camp and they fell into their beds. Victor's body thrashed with pain. He couldn't tell if it was colder outside or inside.

Victor was covered in all of his blankets and wore all of his clothes. His breath turned into white ice in the air. It started to freeze in his lungs. His head spun. His eyes couldn't focus. The white walls thickened with hoary frost, closing in on all sides.

Victor fell into blackness.

Hours later, the trailer door cracked open halfway, then got stuck on the ice. A woman grunted, shoved her way in. She took in the iceberg scene, the frozen waterfall on the sides of the tin camper and Victor lying shaking, half-frozen on his bed, snuggled into Prince.

"Victor!" his wife screamed, then called for Eddie. Eddie stumbled in and the two of them put Victor in his wife's minivan. Victor slurred his speech, saying he couldn't leave. Eddie assured him he would stay.

"You need to get better, Victor, then you can come back," he told him.

Victor's wife took him to Emergency and they wired him up to life-saving equipment. He had pneumonia and his lungs were badly damaged. The doctors said he was near death and had to stay put if he wanted to survive.

He stayed three weeks. A few days into it, he was joined by Eddie. His body had broken down, too, and he too got wired into life-saving machines.

Victor sent his wife out to Africville to take care of the animals.

"Oh, honey. I've got bad news for you," she said, returning to the hospital. "All the animals are dead. Even your dogs are dead," she said, quietly.

Victor ripped the tubes out of his arms and marched out of the hospital in his johnnies. His wife drove him out to Africville. The dogs' bodies were gone, but the ducks and chickens were scattered around the site. He found Walter whimpering nearby. Victor gently pulled the feathers back and saw the big axe hole. The old turkey had been hit, but had run away.

"I can't let Walter suffer like this," Victor murmured to his wife. He found an axe and cut the bird's head off. He wiped back the tears.

The campers were gone, too. Victor and Eddie eventually found them in a Dartmouth incinerator. The campers were broken up and burnt, taking with them all of the brothers' clothes, Victor's guitar, radios – everything. All the artifacts Victor, Eddie and Stephanie had uncovered were gone. All the notebooks Stephanie had kept to detail life on the protest had been burned up. All the photographs she had taken were reduced to ashes.

Eddie went back into the city.

Victor went home.

63

Eddie worked, scrimped and saved for the next year and got enough money to buy another camper. He resumed his protest. The City towed his camper when he was away. He bought another. It was removed. He returned in a tent.

The world braced for the apocalypse as 1999 turned into 2000. It didn't come.

Eddie spent most of his time in Africville, or in town with Stephanie and the twins. Victor joined him when he could, but didn't have the strength to keep sleeping at the protest.

Stephanie came out most weekends and usually brought the kids with her. As the Carverys sat down for a family picnic, it wasn't unusual for motorists to drive by on the bridge ramp, roll down their window and shout, "You niggers go home! You don't belong here!"

Because Stephanie was white, they hated her even more than Eddie. She was used to it. She had been married to a Black man in Montreal and someone spray-painted "Nigger lover" on their apartment door. Sometimes when Eddie and Victor left Africville and she was at the fire alone, cleaning fish, people would stop and throw rocks at her. She was scared. She had cut a hole in the fence between the camp and Bedford Basin so she and Eddie could go swimming. With no showers, it was the best way to keep clean. She figured she could escape in the water, if things got really bad.

One summer night, things got really bad, but she had the kids with her so she couldn't run away. Eddie had gone into town to pick up some KFC for the family picnic. While he was gone, eighteen bikers rumbled by on the bridge. They made such a noise that the kids stared as they passed overhead. The bikers left the bridge and turned down the road to Africville.

The white gang stomped down their kickstands and walked toward Stephanie and her kids, silently surrounding them.

"You go underneath the camper and go let the dogs off," Stephanie whispered to her daughter. To her son, she said, "You just keep screaming and hollering."

She got a third child to light the fire.

"What do you want?" she shouted at the gang.

They didn't answer.

Stephanie's daughter freed the dogs and their snarling teeth drove the men back onto their bikes. They roared off. Eddie returned. They had dinner.

Another night, Stephanie was at the camp by herself when a gang rolled up. They wore black boots and Nazi insignia and glared at her. One reached into his bag, grabbed a weapon Stephanie couldn't identify and pointed it at her.

He fired it with a bang. Stephanie leapt sideways as the missile zoomed in at her, hit the ground and blew up. Fireworks. Another bang. The tent caught fire and quickly burned down.

Stephanie had two big pots of water on the boil and grabbed the cooking sticks, turned them into spears and threw them at the men to keep them at bay.

"I'll dump this boiling water on you if you don't leave!" she shouted.

The gang kept their distance, kept firing the little bombs at her. They left when they were out of ammunition. Stephanie sat on the ground, shaking.

64

One Sunday morning, Eddie walked into town to the Cornwallis Street Baptist Church, stopping at his son's house to shave, clean, comb his hair and put on his good clothes. In church, the minister talked about how parents should get back to physically disciplining their children, that maybe stopping that was harming their upbringing. Spare the rod, spoil the child.

Eddie said no.

The church fell silent and turned to look at him. They had heard him, old Crazy Eddie, speak before, hence the sighs.

"It keeps the violence going," he went on. "I was beat when I was young. My mother was beat. I said I would never beat a woman when I grew up. Well, guess what?"

Eddie explained how he beat his wife because he thought she'd cheated on him, and he thought that gave him the right, if not the duty, to attack her. How the woman was supposed to accept it.

So, he said, everybody should stop beating anybody.

The preacher thanked him, got back to her sermon.

Eddie had arrived at this conclusion after many long, lonely nights in Africville. He had lots of time to think. Stretched out in his sleeping bag, staring up at the stars or the roof of his camper, he thought about when he used drugs and drink, when he used violence. All of the battered faces he had created flowed through his mind and he saw clearly, no longer intoxicated by his rage, the physical, emotional and spiritual damage he had wreaked. Women lying bruised and cut by his hand. Men beaten in bar brawls. He watched himself set himself on fire, shoot drugs into his arms, swallow pills. He saw himself punch, kick and scream at others. He saw how anger and fear were often the same thing.

What was he so afraid of?

Lying alone at night, he tuned his mind movie to his mother getting beaten by his father. He watched himself beat women. He watched himself in bars, fighting, brawling and sprawling unconscious on the floor. He saw Jimmy fall backwards, smoke drifting out of a hole in his chest. He saw his daughter's crying silenced forever.

Why couldn't he stop?

He took the question to a higher power and came up with this: treat other people the way you want to be treated and put God first.

The words of Jesus Christ.

That didn't take away the remorse, but it stopped him adding to it. Or at least slowed him down.

He went to work every day, alone in an abandoned field, holding ground for Africville, dissecting his soul.

Violence was violence and it didn't work, not on Eddie and not on others. This was not some lofty declaration, but a scientific conclusion. Eddie had tested violence extensively, in multiple situations, and it never worked out better for him, or anyone else. One day a man visited his camp and smashed up the boat Eddie kept tied on the shore of the Basin. Eddie used it for fishing and just to get away. Eddie confronted the vandal. The man explained that he was a white supremacist and that the land was public property, so he could do what he pleased. Eddie pointed out the man's car was likewise on public property, so he could do to it what he pleased. Eddie went to his trailer and fetched his axe. He reached the man's car at the same time the man did and shifted the weight of the weapon in his hands. He thought about smashing up the car as the man drove off, but decided not to. Sure, the car would be busted up, but Eddie still wouldn't have a boat. He watched the car speed down the dirt road out of Africville, noted the license plate and reported the incident to the police.

So, along with the drugs and booze, he decided to try to give up his last addiction.

65

In September 2003, the United Nations dispatched Mr. Doudou Diène, Special Rapporteur on contemporary forms of racism, racial discrimination, xenophobia and related intolerance, to Canada. His task was to gauge race relations in Canada, to see how the government dealt with its people and how people dealt with each other, to say what should be done to advance the cause of justice. This was happening everywhere, following the plans laid out at the Durban Conference on racism.

Diène found signs of good work, especially with regards to Aboriginal treaties, but noted, "Canadian society is not free of racial discrimination."

What startled him was official Canada's eagerness to show him what it was doing to combat racism, combined with a denial that there was racism. The gap turned into a chasm when it came to how visible minorities saw their situation. "The contrast between these communities' strong and deep-rooted feelings of discrimination on the one hand and the political will of the federal and provincial authorities on the other indicates a lack of understanding and sympathy as well as poor communication between the communities concerned and the authorities in charge."

The UN's Special Rapporteur toured Canada, meeting with provincial and federal government representatives and people from a range of white and non-white communities. He found both historic and contemporary racism and said a critical part of changing that was "public recognition, at the highest level, of the fact that these evils persist." Educate people. Tell the true story, he urged.

After the Aboriginals discovered, settled and densely populated the Americas with cities and civilizations from perhaps seventy thousand years ago, white people from Britain and France arrived five hundred years ago and brought with them a strong conviction that race was real, that race mattered and that their race was the best of all. That's changed over the years, Diène found, but still, the "'colonial mentality' of those of both British and French descent, who saw themselves as racially superior ... has taken years to erode and, to a lesser extent, still exists."

"A basic precondition for any credible effort to combat racial discrimination is the objective recognition that it really exists," he concluded.

Diène made his way to Nova Scotia in response to a plea from descendants of the African-Canadian community in Nova Scotia to tell the story of Africville.

In his official 2004 report for the UN, Diène dates Africville's origins back to the 1700s, when it was founded by slaves brought by white people, by Maroons and by Black Loyalists fleeing the revolutionary and racist United States as liberated slaves – by the men and women who built Halifax.

He reported on the devaluing of Africville from 1913 to 1973, with industrial growth coming at the expense of the residents of Africville: the bone-meal plant, the cotton factory, the rolling mill/nail factory, the slaughterhouse and the port facility for handling coal. And of course, in the 1950s, the City dump.

Diène found that as early as 1915, the City had made explicit its intent to take the land of Africville. By 1960, the City embarked on an urban renewal campaign, forcibly displacing the residents of Africville to make room for industrial expansion. "After 150 years of collusion between the provincial government and the business community, including through abuse of power, neglect, encroachment and invasion of hazardous industrial materials, in 1970 all of the community was forcefully removed without proper compensation," he concluded.

He made no bones about it: "The case of Africville is emblematic of the past condition of people of African descent in Nova Scotia. The Black community in Nova Scotia faces numerous challenges, including the overrepresentation in prisons, a dependence on the welfare system and increase of representation in low-income housing and other problems in the criminal justice system.

"The cultural depth of racism also colours the deepest layers of the emotions and sensitivities of discriminatory experience. Like most countries, Canada does not appear to have grasped the magnitude of this submerged part of the racist iceberg. And yet it is only by taking account of this intangible dimension of racism, through an appropriate intellectual and ethical strategy, that it will be possible in the longer term, with the help of legal strategy, to ensure the eradication of racism and discrimination."

The United Nations report praised Canada for much of its work improving race relations and righting past wrongs, but drew its attention to "a number of shortcomings." Chief among these was Africville. The United Nations called on Nova Scotia to "re-examine the conditions of their relocation, particularly from Africville, taking particular account of their situation regarding human rights and economic and social conditions with a view to granting them reparation."

The report was received by the City, province and federal government and gently filed in that special filing can for all things Africville.

66

Eddie's friend Rocky Jones was set to come out and visit him. It was mid-winter around 2004 and it was cold. Eddie tidied up the camp and got ready for company. Not many people made it down the road to visit him in winter. He was excited.

A blizzard blew into the city, paralyzing it.

Night came and Eddie fell asleep waiting for his friend. He was out of fuel and he may as well have sat in the open fields. The snow slipped into the camper, wrapping Eddie in its icy blanket. It drifted under him, over his hands, his face, his hair, his legs, his chest. The rain came and froze it there when the temperature dropped.

Eddie woke up, tried to sit up, but couldn't move. He fought panic, twisted and turned his body for thirty minutes until he slowly generated enough heat and friction to break the ice's glue between his backside and the bed. Getting up took the skin off his shoulders and the backs of his legs. His mouth and eyes were frozen shut, as snot and tears had leaked out and turned his beard and eyelashes to ice. It hurt just to open them. He was so cold, he started to feel hot and tore off all of his clothes. He sat naked in his camper, shivering in the hallucinatory heat.

Rocky, then a high-profile lawyer, made it out in the morning. He had to park his car way down at Barrington Street and walk in. Where the plowing ended, Africville began. He tromped in through the snow and found Eddie in a desperate state. He dug him out. Why not come back to the city? Plenty of places to stay.

Eddie shook his head. His friend got more fuel and thawed out the camper.

67

Eddie got a second-hand kerosene heater. He filled it up and turned it on, drifting off in the peaceful heat. The heater was on the counter, so he could look at the flame inside as he fell asleep.

The fire flickered on the wick.

Eddie's eyes grew heavy.

The flame twisted.

The room was hot.

Eddie fell toward sleep.

The flame fell toward the floor.

Eddie woke up groggily, watching the fire spread in a puddle on the camper floor. With a whoosh! it exploded into the camper. Eddie was wide awake now and engulfed in flames. He leapt out of bed, grabbed the heater and raced out the door and the fire came with him. Outside, he beat the flames dead on him and tried to save the camper. It was well ablaze and both canvas ends burned up in a flurry of red on a white winter's day. When the flames finally gave up, the inside was scorched and Eddie was homeless again.

He went into the city. Worked odd jobs to earn money. Got another camper. Went back to Africville.

68

Eddie turned sixty in 2006. For Eddie, the whole decade was a lesson in all the ways the world can break your heart.

The first lesson came on a Christmas Day. He'd gone into the city to spend it with Eddie Junior and his family – including his grandson, Eddie Leo Carvery III. Eddie's heart swelled with pride, and then with ill health. He was on new medication and thought maybe that was causing the pain sweeping through the left side of his chest. He breathed. Tried to stay calm. He knew it was a heart attack, but what could he do? If his time was up, his time was up. The intense pain passed enough that he could ask his son to drive him to the hospital, which he did. While the doctors were working out what to do with him, he had another heart attack.

The next Christmas he had two more heart attacks. His son rushed him to hospital again and the doctors patched him up and sent him home. He went home, but his camper had vanished yet again.

He got another. Resumed the protest.

The next year, another heart attack. It only felt like bad gas that time. He didn't worry. God would stop his heart when He was ready and nothing in the world could kill him before then.

In the brightly lit hospital, the doctor shook his head in amazement.

"What?" Eddie asked him, adjusting his hospital gown.

The doctor told him a vein that ran over his heart had popped loose and fallen below his heart.

"Is that a bad thing?" Eddie asked.

The doctor shook his head. It was a natural bypass. No need for surgery.

"It is so remarkable. I've read about it, but never witnessed it," he said.

"So my heart's okay?"

The doctor looked at him over the clipboard.

"Let me put it this way. If you were getting on the highway and there were three roads – one going to Prince Edward Island, one to New Brunswick and one to Nova Scotia – you'd have to stay in Nova Scotia. The other roads are blocked. In fact, you can't even drive on the main roads in Nova Scotia."

So Eddie stuck to the backroads of his heart.

Toward the end of the decade, he had more heart problems. Stephanie ended things with him. It had been a long time – nearly twenty years – but she couldn't handle life with the Hundingo Man any more. He was getting worse – nasty, ill-tempered and hateful, was how she put it. And violent. The man she'd left in Montreal had beat her, and she wasn't going to let it happen again. The double life was taking a toll, too. At home, Eddie was Eddie and everything was fine. Out there, he was the Hundingo Man. She had to put the kids first. Not the protest, not Africville, but the children. So she ended it. It didn't end in violence, anyway. That was a first for Eddie. He didn't try to kill himself, or her. Instead, after the heartbreak, he could quietly thank her for the great sacrifice she'd made to the protest. To him.

"She was very brave to stay with me all that time."

69

On a warm August day in 2009, Eddie and Victor sat in the old courtyard to the school in the middle of a half-circle of campers. Spike, Eddie's ferocious baby of a dog, sat in the shade. Victor strummed an old guitar, singing softly while Eddie talked about how teachers used to always chide him for procrastinating. Squinting his eyes in the bright sunlight, Eddie decided he was grateful to Mrs. Beck for branding him a procrastinator all those years ago.

"Forty-some years later, I'm still sitting in Africville procrastinating. I can't move on till this thing gets made right, and I can maybe have a little bit of life. There should be a capital sign over my head called FAILURE," he mused. "It's the way the cards were dealt. I've taken this thing called failure and turned it around and to me, it sounds like success."

Trucks rattled past along the access road that ran a few feet from Eddie's house. The train tracks were just beyond that. In the grassy field next to their compound, Victor had erected a makeshift shrine on the grounds of the church. Eddie had a camper again, a new one parked next to the burnt-out one, which now served as a storage unit. There was a big new trailer in the lot, too – Nelson Carvery had parked it there in the summer to throw his weight behind Eddie's protest. He didn't sleep there, but he did come out to check on Eddie when he could.

Earlier that month, at the Africville reunion, the City renamed the access road Africville Road. The press release was ecstatic, but Eddie was not.

"Forty years ago, they were saying the same thing: 'Oh, next year we're going to do this, and next year we're going to do that.' Just be quiet and don't say nothing," he told a reporter who had wandered over to his camp. "We had our own church, which they tore down at three in the morning ... what they done to us was barbaric. It's an endless story of betrayal. They got their container pier – that's a billion-dollar industry, and it's ours. They've got houses from Lady Hammond Road right across to Barrington Street, but not one Black person from Africville lives in any of them. Everybody admits that Halifax was wrong and racist in the 1960s and I suggest to you that it's still just as bad as it was in the '60s, because they have not addressed us as a community. We have not received an apology – we demand a public inquiry."

Eddie still demanded a public inquiry. People still wanted to get paid for the land taken from them. The church, for which Martin Luther King III broke the soil in 1992, seventeen years ago, was still not there.

Three weeks after the reunion finished, Eddie and Victor were back on their own in Africville. Dump trucks moved a pile of dirt from one spot to another. A driver honked his horn and Eddie waved.

"My life has ... I've never accomplished anything," he sighed. Victor kept strumming, singing softly. "Nothing. I've done a lot of things. I've met so many extraordinary people. I used to be illiterate. I don't believe I'm illiterate now. When the community was here, it was my world. We didn't go into town for nothing – "

Eddie's thoughts were interrupted by a van pulling into his dirt driveway. It was his friend Craig Vemb, son of Curley, the man who famously advised a cop that if he pulled his trigger to shoot Curley's dog, Curley would pull his own trigger. Craig was stopping by to help fix the generator that conked out last winter, leaving Eddie with no electricity and therefore no heat. He didn't have running water or sewage, either. Just like the old days in Africville. City services have always ended with the pavement.

"I'm not sure I've got another winter in me," Eddie said as Craig opened up the generator. Protest winters are massive, snow-topped mountains that can only be climbed with pure will. The thinly walled camper, wide open to oceanic winds, offers little protection, even with bales of hay strapped to the side. As the snow piles up, the house gets colder and colder. The world gets smaller, too, as Eddie can't go sit in the park, or wander around Africville – not unless he wants to shiver for the rest of the night.

Eddie had a new place in town via Social Services, an apartment in the North End, but he stayed out in Africville. Night after night, day after day, winter after winter. Warmth, a bed, food and cable TV were a thirty-minute walk down the road, but the lure of the cold, abandoned land was stronger.

Craig declared the generator dead. Eddie took the news in stride. They sat on plastic chairs in Eddie's front yard and talked about the struggle. At first, Craig interjected and objected to Eddie's take on things, but soon fell silent, falling under the preacher's spell. Eddie knew the past and the present and had big dreams for the future. His friend sat back, head on his hands, eyes on Eddie, listening.

The conversation was interrupted by a film crew. A reporter from a local news station was there with Juanita Peters, who had just made *Can't Stop Now*, a documentary about Africville. Eddie's in it, shivering in the dark of another Africville winter. They wanted to talk to Eddie for a show about it for the upcoming Atlantic Film Festival. Eddie thought for a second, then nodded yes.

"What should I say?" he asked Craig and Victor. Craig and Victor gave him lots of ideas: tell them your piece, say what you say in church, tell them about Africville. Eddie thought it over, combed his hair and beard for the TV crew.

70

Irvine Carvery is in the movie, too. He talks about his undying dreams for Africville. Later, he spelled out what he wants in that church built to replace the one bulldozed in his childhood.

"We need to have an institution that talks about our rich history, that talks about our contribution as a people to this society. Men and women from Africville helped build this city, helped build this province. They built the railroads, they worked the docks, they served in every great conflict this country participated in, some paying the ultimate price," he said. "That connection to the larger society needs to be told."

That optimism came in 2009, seventeen years after the church was first not built, more than forty years after the City tore it down in the middle of the night.

"We want to have a space where like stories can be told. Not just Africville, but if there's a story somewhere in the world that's similar to what happened in Africville, let's tell it in that space."

Irvine waxed poetic, seeing the resurrected church as a place for deep healing – for the City and Africville. It could host burials, marriages for Africvillians and exhibits about other dispossessed people who met indignity with dignity.

His optimism dimmed when his thoughts turned to his brother.

"If I could have found a way to make this all Eddie's idea, and have Eddie involved in the society, then there wouldn't be this issue, this separate issue," he reflected. "But it's not and that might be the core to some of the difficulties we're having in agreeing that we agree."

Life worked out well for Irvine. He was still president of the Africville Genealogy Society, still married with a big, happy family in a nice home. He was a manager with a City organization that helps people find housing. He was also recently elected as head of Halifax's school board, the first African-Nova Scotian to hold that position. He got it a few days after Barack Obama was elected president of a slightly larger organization. In 2010, he was inducted into the W.P. Oliver Wall of Honour at the Black Cultural Centre in Dartmouth.

"People need to be given an opportunity to heal. There's still a lot of hurt around the whole question of Africville. Eddie probably epitomizes that hurt," Irvine said, sitting in his North End office. "I think Eddie has too much time on his hands. He thinks too much about it – continually, all the time. He doesn't have anything else in his life. It's just this, this focus on this. It's not healthy. Sure, stay passionate about Africville, but get some balance in your life. But we need to get the question of Africville solved."

Irvine still dreamed of the church, of a tangible sign of Africville reborn. Perhaps they could hold a healing circle, with help from his Mi'kmaq roots. It was time for peace and reconciliation, he said.

"Not just for people from Africville, but anybody involved in the destruction of our community. Whether they were actively involved, or stood on the sidelines while it happened, give them an opportunity to come into the circle and talk it. Get it off your chest: say it, with no repercussions. We just want you to tell your story and have it recorded, but no legal ramifications – nothing more than talking. Get rid of that pain and that hurt, because it's negative and negative energy is not good. It'll kill you."

Irvine was also still Eddie's younger brother. Eddie, Victor, Irvine and their sister Priscilla were all that remained of Daisy and Clarence's family. Eddie and Irvine rarely spoke to each other, but they spoke well of each other.

"He's a character. He'll go down in folklore – his persona will only grow as people retell the stories of Eddie Carvery," Irvine concluded, smiling.

71

The Hundingo Man took a visitor on a summer tour of Africville. Passing through a black gate into Seaview Memorial Park, he described the buildings demolished forty years ago as though they were still standing. You could almost hear children laughing, splashing into the water, old folks rocking on their front porch and the church bell ringing.

A group of people sat on the hill in the middle of the park, chatting as their dogs bounded around the field. Spike, Eddie's dog, ran over to play. Eddie started reeling off names, pointing to ghost buildings. This family lived here, that family there. Who had a big happy family, who had a troubled life. Who died. Who lived. Who never married. Who had a shop. Whose house caught fire and burned to the ground, killing the children, and how the fire department never showed up. Where the in-home businesses were, where Granny Pink's house was and what it looked like.

At the far end of the park, kids played on the swings and slides. That was Joe Skinner's house. Beyond that, the same road there today was there in Africville, still connecting its unpaved world to the paved world beyond.

Tired, Eddie sat down on a bench. Spike lay at his feet. Eddie spoke about Africville as the late-summer sun filtered through the trees. How Africvillians were raised to face that world of pavement: a world where power was far away, a tale of two cities that lived separate lives until the City decided it was time to pave a one-way street to integration, how Africvillians struggled to stay afloat in the new immersion.

A woman walked into the park, pulled by two dogs. The big one flew at the end of his leash like a kite on a windy day. He pulled the woman to Eddie and Spike hopped to his feet protectively. The dogs sniffed each other and the yellow visiting dog growled. Spike snarled and soon the two were fighting. Eddie shouted at Spike, the woman shouted at her dog. Eddie grabbed the visitor by its harness and pulled it off. He scolded Spike, who whimpered and backed off.

"I'm so sorry!" the woman said, being pulled off by her dog again. Eddie walked with her, chatted with her, then she headed into the park. No harm. No hard feelings. He sat back down on the bench and resumed his narrative.

A little later, a warden walked into the park. Eddie sniffed him out instantly. The warden walked off toward the opposite end of the park, looked in Eddie's direction for a while, but then turned his attention inward, sipping his coffee.

Eddie fell back into Africville.

The warden returned.

"Doing a little interview?" he asked, nodding at the digital recorder in the visitor's hand.

Eddie nodded, his face darkened with distrust.

"I'm just curious," the park warden added. "I notice your dog's not on a leash."

Eddie and Spike got their hackles up.

"What park are we in, buddy?" Eddie asked.

"Seaview Park," the warden answered.

"Is this not an off-leash park?" Eddie asked.

"Have a look at the signage – " the warden started, pointing to the off-leash sign nailed to a tree six feet from where Eddie and Spike sat.

"Are you going to do this to me?" Eddie argued, agitated. "I live here."

"I know," the warden continued. "Have a look at the sign."

"I'm not visiting – I was born right here," Eddie said, pointing to the field behind him that once held his family home.

"Yes, sir," the warden said.

"I'm not bothering a soul."

"Do you abide by the laws of the park?" the warden asked.

"I try to. I do very well," Eddie answered.

"Okay. Well, the rules of the park are right over there, as clear as can be on the sign."

"Buddy," Eddie said, angry. "Listen, I'm going to ask you something. Are you going to give me a ticket? Did you come way out here to bother me because I'm two feet on the other side?"

"Sir."

"Please don't do this. It's not nice. Come on, buddy," Eddie said to his visitor, getting up and leaving. Spike followed.

"Get away from me, man. I'm so fed up with your bullshit," Eddie called over his shoulder to the warden. "Come way the fuck out here, talking shit to me. You better go do your job. Fuck off. Go do your job."

The warden stood still, scowling.

"This is not your job. Now fuck off! You deserve to get punched in your mouth," Eddie muttered, walking off.

"This is what I have to put up with. I'm short-tempered because I know their purpose is just to harass me," he apologized to his visitor.

Eddie walked home in a foul mood, a storm on a sunny day. His mood brightened when he saw old friends from Africville sitting outside his camper, waiting for him.

Twenty minutes later, an unmarked police car and marked police van pulled up. An officer got out of the first. Four burly young cops wearing mirrored sunglasses piled out of the second.

They surrounded Eddie, walled him off from his friends. The cops asked him something. He answered in anger. The cops turned outward, interrogating Eddie's friends.

Eddie thought it was about the dog and so defended himself. The head cop made it clear he was there because the warden had phoned the police, alleging Eddie Carvery had threatened to assault him.

For a second, Eddie looked like he was going to blow. Then, he recalculated, started smiling, and charmed the cops. He smiled, teased the officers, flattered them by saying they surely have more important things to do. If they want to arrest him, arrest him. If they want to ticket him, ticket him. The cops weren't eager to make anything official out of it, though one handed around cards with incident numbers on them. Eddie told them about Africville and the protest, invited them to join him.

Everybody laughed.

"Now, did you threaten to hit that man?" the head cop asked, smiling at Eddie like he was a naughty boy.

"Well, maybe I did," Eddie played along, putting on a mischievous grin. "I just said he deserved to get hit, not that I was going to do it!"

The cop laughed.

"Well, just don't do that again," he said, smiling behind his mirrored sunglasses.

The cops joshed with Eddie for a while, warned him again, then piled into the van and car and drove off.

A few minutes later, animal control arrived, also summoned by the warden. The driver, a podgy young white man, took a verbal barrage from Victor, who had arrived late on the scene and started sticking up for his brother. Eddie had had his dogs taken before and had no money to get Spike out of the pound. The driver raised his hands and made it clear he thought the warden was a dick and he just wanted to tell Eddie the woman with the dogs hadn't called the police.

The animal control man left. Eddie and his friends walked down to the water. The woman with the dogs came out of the park, saw Eddie and his friends standing together by the water. She hesitated, then walked across the vacant lot and spoke to Eddie. She wanted him to know she hadn't called the cops. Eddie said he knew she hadn't. They chatted for a while and he invited her to visit him any time she was in Africville. She promised to and walked back into the park, glancing over her shoulder at the Hundingo Man.

Eddie chatted with his old friends on the shores of Africville.

72

The hardest years were when nobody knew he was there. Nobody cared what he was doing. He was just a homeless guy in the park. A squatter. It hurt outside, but it healed inside. He wasn't built to thrive in the city. He was built for Africville.

Standing in Africville, he knew his place and time. He knew he had a worth. He knew his people had a worth. When he started on that path in 1970, he had imagined the fight would be short, victory easy. He was a young man, full of strength, but victory proved elusive. As he became an old man, alone in Africville, he realized the fight would last as long as it lasted.

Others joined him. For a weekend, a week, a month, a decade. They left. The talk is easy, the walk almost impossible. Eddie walked on with no victory line in view, only more horizon.

Any time he gave up, a darkness churned up his insides. He'd hear his mother and grandmother calling to him from the grave of Africville and return to their land.

He learned about the official City history and how his people were blacked out of it. They were a distinct society, but they wouldn't become an extinct society. Not on his watch. He wanted to build the Black space in the city's collective mind.

He had a job to do and he'd do it till it was done. Or until he was done.

The world changed around him. Africvillians moved on with their lives, had kids, grandkids. The United States blew up over racism, then put itself back together again with the Civil Rights Movement. South

Africa ended Apartheid, Nelson Mandela finished his long walk to freedom and became president. The U.S. elected a Black president.

Eddie kept walking.

The City stole his homes, his property, everything he had, over and over and over again. They took nothing. Eddie regrouped and returned to the protest. He was shot at. He stood his ground. His family was firebombed. He didn't back down.

The destruction of Africville was wrong and he would walk until it was made right.

"I can see them fixing Africville and I can see them fixing the rest of the problems, because it's not our problem to inherit. Somebody did something wrong and they messed up our system. They gave us the face of a racist and we don't deserve it because we're Canadians and we're all colours. That's the good part about us – we don't tolerate racism, because that's bullshit," he said as evening fell, darkening the Basin and the green fields.

The European forefathers who brought racism to Canada were wrong, he said.

"You're on the wrong horse. You're in the wrong country. What you did was wrong, when you brought those people here in slavery. What they did in servitude, they dug out them streets, they hold a position in this country called Canada. These people should have a role of prominence. We should pay homage and say, 'Wow, what a fascinating country we've got. These people gave it to us, they carved out the roads, let's make this a beautiful history.'

"We can get everybody in this boat. We're the Canadians!"

His voice rose passionately as the caul descended, allowing Eddie to see what was beyond the veil of ordinary life.

"This gives you pride that you feel deep down in your soul and makes you feel like you're gonna last forever, because you got a worth, you got a value. That's what the protest has done for me. I was broke in the city. I was a broken man. I came to Africville, I prayed so hard, I was so completely broke, I asked God to pick me up. I didn't want to be the liar I was when I walked out of the city. I was everything to everybody, but to myself, my own worst enemy. I was creating no solutions, just problems. I took a look at myself and put a worth on myself and I didn't feel very good about it. I felt like I was the worst human being in the world and I deserved all these bad things happening to me. When I started fighting for Africville, it changed me. I stopped being the centre of attraction for me. I learned to put me far from Eddie. I distanced myself from me, because this me I knew was selfish. He was addicted. I couldn't trust him. He was broke. I started getting well, through fasting, through abstinence.

"I'm guilty as sin about everything. I'm not the best guy in the world for this job. The Lord could have picked somebody a little more respectable, with a good reputation, but I'm the guy that was broke, I'm the guy that went down the road, I'm the guy that Jesus said 'Hey' to. He did that with Paul, too. Paul used to take the Christians and kill them. Paul was bad. Jesus came to him and changed him.

"Since I been out here, I learned what discipline is, because you have to be very disciplined to be here. I've learned what it is to be patient. I realized how long a winter's night is, and the extent of the rain. Stuff that I never thought about, I've had time to think about."

Eddie fell silent. He watched the golden sunlight fade in the darkening Basin as the earth turned from its star, facing the endless shadows of space.

73

White smoke billowed out of chimneys in Uniacke Square. Broad winter sunlight filled the blue sky over the snow-covered landscape. It was February 2010 and the temperature dropped to –14°C in the daytime. When the wind hit, the temperature fell to –24°C. Few people ventured out. Two women bundled in dark coats walked a tiny dog. Even the dog was wrapped in a pink sweater. A white field opened up north of the Square, the snow sparkling like it was hiding diamonds. Small Black children packed into thick snowsuits and heavy toques held hands with their parents as they walked home from school. A few stopped to slide down the hills, but no one was braving the playground. The brick George Dixon Centre sat at the top of the field. This was Stephanie Sparks's view, but she was trying to change it. She loved the house she was in, but it was a high-crime area and she didn't feel safe.

Eddie's apartment was a few streets up, on Maynard Street, in a new grey building. Irvine's house was on the same street, where he lived with his wife Monica and where they raised Irvine, Shaun and Monique. Victor, father of Quincey, Bonnie, Victor, Tina, Jason and Justin, lived in the same neighbourhood, in a blue house with his wife Valerie and their cats. Nelson lived in a pink house on Creighton Street with his wife, Linda Carvery. She was a federal judge and a jazz singer. Art still flowed out of Africville. In the last few years, there was *Don't Stop Now*, the documentary about Nelson, Eddie and Irvine, a couple of children's books, an academic book called *Razing Africville: a Geography of Racism* and, a few years before that, a masterful CD by jazz musician Joe Sealy called *Africville Suite*. He won a Juno for the album inspired by the death of his father, an Africvillian.

Dawn lived a short walk away. She volunteered at the local food bank. She and Eddie saw each other once in a while, flipping through old photos, talking about old times in a curious mix of familiarity and awkwardness – like an old married couple on their first date. Lately, Eddie was helping her paint her house. Eddie's surviving children, including Denise, Eddie Junior, Randy, Dinki, Theresa, Chantel, Tandra and the twins, lived in the North End or scattered elsewhere.

The Angus L. Macdonald Bridge touched down just beyond Uniacke Square, leapt across the Halifax Harbour to Dartmouth, busy with rush-hour traffic. Down below, Barrington Street ran along the water. Head south and it would take you to the heart of the city. Head north and it took you to Africville. Houses lined the left of the road out of town, single-family units giving way to Mulgrave Park's denser public housing before yielding to scattered small houses. On the right, an industrial landscape interrupted the view of the water: piers, shipping yards, garages. Signs promised new condominium buildings on the left and further down they delivered with a big building sitting on a spot near where the *Mont Blanc* blew up all those years ago, devastating the North End in the 1917 Halifax Explosion. Up ahead, the A. Murray MacKay Bridge rumbled with trucks and cars. It was named after a chairman of the bridge commission, but some people thought it should be named after the land it took. The Africville Bridge.

Barrington Street turned into an on-ramp flanked by billboards, but a lightly marked road broke off to the right. A big white sign with a circle painting of water and land welcomed visitors to Seaview Park. Underneath, a smaller, newer sign said, Welcome to Africville. The rusty metal was bolted to the wood, the letters popped out like stencils. The snowy road broke right, making a tricky crossing over the train tracks and two industrial roads used by fast-driving eighteen-wheelers. Drivers had to move quickly to skirt across the danger zones, but then Africville Road bore left, cutting under the bridge. Carry on and it went to the dockyards, but turn right into a parking lot and visitors could stop their cars on Kildare Field.

A chain-link fence opened to an icy, untended park. Drifts of snow matched the drifts of land. The fence ran right along the water. Where the path rose above the water – that's where Africville's shoreline once ran. More rusted metal signs in the park told visitors where Skinner's Well was, and Tibby's Pond. That sign was stuck in the middle of the field and no-

body explained how it was ever a pond. Copses of trees wore snow like a prom dress. Four barking dogs played in the centre of the park while four owners huddled in the shrinking patches of sunlight.

An iron gate marked the far end of the park. A sign on top of it informed visitors that bylaw P-600 closed the park from ten p.m. to five a.m. every day. No sleeping here. A dirt road connected the small, secondary parking area to Africville Road. To the right, open dirt land stretched to the water. Eddie's Medicine Wheel poked out of the snow. The carefully arranged collection of rocks, driftwood, feathers and a small bird skull was his latest building project. To the left, a driveway next to a white picket fence and shrubs led to a small compound. A big trailer sat to the left, a small green-and-white camper straight ahead. Next was a burnt-out trailer with "Africville Protest" written on its wooden sides in red paint. Eddie's camper sat beside it and a new shed beside that. Lots of houses, but only one resident. At Christmas, Eddie hoisted an inflatable Santa Claus on top of the shed. In January, he replaced it with a snowman.

Spike ran barking to greet visitors. If it was a stranger, he kept barking, pushing them off his master's land. If it was a friend, he turned into a quivering puppy, begging to be patted.

A pot-bellied stove sat in the middle of the trailers, puffing white smoke and a little heat into a day so cold exposed skin was damaged in minutes. Eddie sat inside the trailer. He had fuel for the day, so the open flame on the stove and the blocked-off windows kept it comfortably warm. It was small – a bed that converted into a table, a bench with room for one and a busted chair for a second visitor. A few books lay open on the bed – the Bible, a book on the Halifax Explosion, one about Mi'kmaq spirituality and Malcolm X's autobiography. Eddie watched a TV balanced on the sink. *The Oprah Winfrey Show* was on.

As the long, hard winter of 2009-2010 settled over Halifax and Africville, Eddie made the difficult decision to start spending nights in his city apartment. "I've got to preserve myself as long as I can," he explained apologetically. "This job is far from over."

His son, Eddie Junior, picked him up every day at six a.m. and drove his father to work before going to work himself. Eddie Junior owned a painting business and lived in town with his family. The Hundingo Man didn't take weekends or holidays off. He was at the protest Christmas Day and New Year's Day, too. Eddie stayed deep into the darkness, catching a ride back into town at the end of the day. If no one picked him up, he got on his old, clunky red bike and pedalled into town, wearing a hard hat for protection. Food came from the food bank or friends. Sometimes it didn't come at all.

"I can go days without eating and not realize how hungry I am until I do eat," he reflected one day when a visitor brought lunch.

In early February, Eddie was asked to address the TYP class at Dalhousie University. He hadn't been on campus since he dropped out of the program in its first year in 1970. The dozen Black and Mi'kmaq students listened raptly as he told them about Africville, about the destruction of Africville, and about the steady shrinking of Black and Mi'kmaq space in Canada's collective mind. Just as most maps of the world literally shrink Africa, so too the history books reduce the achievements of Black people in Canada.

"People want to let that segment of our society die. I'm not prepared to do that. It's our space – the Black space. We earned it as Canadians. Our ancestors paid the price and today we are excluded from history. This is my life. This is my job. If I don't do it, I feel like I'm betraying myself and my purpose," he said to explain his forty years in the wilderness to the young students.

He wondered who he would have been, what he would have accomplished, had he stayed away from the drugs. More painfully, he wondered what the protest could have accomplished if he'd had a better reputation. Maybe then people would have listened to him.

After his talk, he was surrounded by the students. Everyone wanted to shake his hand, thank him. One of the young men was descended from Africvillians. Eddie remembered his family, his house, out in Africville.

"For most people, a will is what they leave behind. For him, a will is what keeps him there," marvelled another man.

As the protest entered its fortieth year, the little white camper entered its third year as Eddie's home. It was small and dirty, but comfortable. Yesterday's talk had him thinking about his own TYP experience. The timing was all wrong for him, but he wished the new students well. He remembered one TYP history professor who introduced him to Black history and inspired him to fight racism. He remembered his mother, a proud Mi'kmaq woman, proud of her son.

So what would twenty-three-year-old Eddie have thought of sixty-three-year-old Eddie? Would he still have started the protest? "I don't think I could have survived that," Eddie said. It was only supposed to last a few months, maybe a year, but it didn't work out like that. The community he tried to raise stayed away. Instead, a container pier had grown up on Africville land. A dog park. Long before that, a whole neighbourhood called Fairview moved onto Africville farmland. The prison. The hospital. Physical Africville was shrunk to the land Eddie occupied.

"I feel that my life that I spent out here on this protest, it's been such a waste of my life, because I'm looking around and saying, who benefited? What did I accomplish? And to me, I didn't do what I wanted to. I didn't do what I set out to do, never even come close," he sighed, staring at his hands. Uncelebrated, unwritten, unsung, but unbending.

"What I went through out here, it was a transformation. I was stripped of everything I believed in, everything I thought was right, and then I had to reconnect my bones and put myself back together."

He studied the Halifax Explosion. The North End was destroyed, but the City and the world beyond poured millions into its rebirth. When the City drew a circle on a map marking the area it would rebuild, that circle included Africville. The next day the City redrew the circle, leaving Africville on the outside. Within a few years, the beautiful, modern Hydrostone housing was built in the North End. More housing and businesses followed. It became a vibrant, economically thriving, culturally distinct area. Africville continued to be ignored.

Eddie imagined a City that had opted to invest that $800,000 in upgrading Africville, not destroying it. He saw a bustling waterside town, full of happy homes and thriving businesses. A funky cultural mecca, a must-see on any tourist's trip to Halifax.

"We could have had a home for a home, and they still could have all their homes. They still could have their bridge and their container pier," he said. "It would have made all the difference in the world. We would have homes. We would have futures."

What would Eddie Carvery be doing?

He'd be a community organizer. Leading Africville, just like he was then. Only with other people following him.

"That's just a dream," he sighed.

The destruction of Africville blew the foundations out from under his people and shattered their dreams. Forty years later, people are still struggling to rebuild after losing everything families had built for generations. Equity, education, economic power, all wiped out. A home for a loan.

"It's made us second-class citizens, beggars. Our inheritance demands that that should never have happened to us. They decided we weren't worth it. They took us as a people and destroyed us, as a community they raped us, as a society they killed us. I don't understand how that could happen in this country in this day and age. How could there be a genocide? There was a Black space," Eddie said.

The physical landscape and the spiritual landscape was and should once again be Black, but history had been blacked out.

The blight was not on Africville. The blight was on Halifax.

The first Africville church was way up on the hill. The second Africville church, the one torn down in the middle of the night, the one being rebuilt any day now, sat in front of Eddie's camp. A rusty metal sign marked the spot. That, and the shrine Victor built.

Eddie liked the idea of rebuilding a memorial church. But why stop there? Why not have an active church? And why stop there? Why not build an interpretive centre? And why stop there? Why not build houses?

Bring the children of Africville home. Africville reborn, a living symbol of Black strength. Halifax reborn, too, finally waking up from the nightmare of history. It was wrong. Let's make it right. Halifax as a byword for enlightenment, a global inspiration for deep justice.

In forty years, Eddie beat speed, beat crack, beat alcoholism and beat violence. He beat self-loathing and found he had a worth. For the last year of the protest, he had been sober, single and sane.

"I never thought I'd ever be at the point where I could sit up and hold a conversation with another person. My addiction had me so sick I couldn't use my hands to write, I couldn't talk a conversation. I was so paranoid, everyone was an authority out to get me. I was almost crazy. I was crazy," he reflected. "I had to change me. I had a bleeding heart, I felt all this great pity for me and woe is me. I had to get away from that. I've grown. I've become a person of conscience. This protest saved me."

He turned his thoughts outward, to the Africville diaspora, to Black people across the country.

"I see us being lost as a culture, as a people who contributed to Canada. It's evolved from being not just about Africville. It's about a space, a feeling toward a congregation in our community, and it's a Black congregation, and it's where we're placed on the ladder in this society. We need to reform this society and include everybody. We're losing that space. Even though we're growing in population, we're shrinking in size of community, of space."

Eddie dreamed of living in a house in Africville. Maybe with running water, electricity and even paved roads. "Basically, I ain't never left Africville. I got no intention on leaving Africville."

It wasn't the money he was after, though reparations were due. It was dignity.

"I don't think this job is over. I think this job's just begun. The thing that's got to come is a sense of pride, a sense that what happened has got to be corrected so we can move forward."

He figured the City was just waiting for the old hermit in the camper to die and hoping Africville died with him. Africville was founded in the 1700s. Eddie brought it into the twenty-first century. As long as his heart beats, it will beat in Africville. In the foundations of his hopeful soul he believes that one day, people will do the right thing.

If he walks long enough.

74

The packed meeting at the North End YMCA was tense. People were angry. It had been forty-five years since the City bulldozed their homes and feelings were as raw as burnt skin. The mayor was there. The premier of Nova Scotia, too, plus the media. Eddie Carvery was there. It was February 2010.

"Praise the Lord!" shouted Rhonda Britton, minister of the Cornwallis Street Baptist Church. She spoke about the wounds warriors bear, the losses they suffer. The hundred seated people cheered. A dozen at the back looked on sternly, arms folded. "We as a community today can shout victory, hallelujah!"

"No. We haven't won," a man from the back shouted.

"Yes, we have – as a community, we have won," Britton said.

The crowd cheered. The men at the back shook their heads angrily.

Britton ramped up the preaching. The applause drowned out the boos.

"We can't feed our children the bitter pills – we must give them the pills of love!"

The preacher sat down to loud cheers and Amens.

The night before, Halifax's City Council had voted to approve a settlement it had made with the Africville Genealogy Society. It was supposed to resolve the 1995 lawsuit. Nobody had said what the deal was and when a woman asked after the cryptic vote, council shut itself down.

The mayor, Peter Kelly, promised to apologize on February 24. He sat at the front of the gym with the other dignitaries. Three days earlier, a Black man and his white wife in rural Nova Scotia had awoken to screams of "Die, nigger, die!" and went outside to find a seven-foot cross burning in the night. A noose hung around the crossbeams. The man sent his wife and their five children to a hotel and vowed to move as soon as he could sell the house. An article in *The Globe and Mail* called Nova Scotia the "Mississippi of the North" above a photograph of the makeshift cross Victor Carvery had erected on the site of the long-demolished church at the Africville protest site. The rural community, white and Black, had rallied around the family. The father of the accused cross-burners appeared shocked and crying on the national news, asking for forgiveness.

At the North End YMCA, speaker after speaker rose to lament the murder of Africville. Never again, they said, never again. We can become better because of this. We can do the right thing.

Kelly was called to the podium. The crowd fell silent as the slight man with dark hair and deep eyes cleared his throat. "You need to have someone from government stand before you, look you in the eye, and say, 'We are sorry,'" he said. He spoke of urban renewal, of the destruction of worlds.

"All our histories have been forever altered because of the loss of Africville," Kelly said.

"Give it back," an unmistakable voice demanded from the back of the room.

Eddie Carvery. Wearing a Che Guevera t-shirt and watching closely.

Kelly continued, reading the formal apology.

"On behalf of the Halifax Regional Municipality, I apologize to the former Africville residents and their descendants for what they have endured for almost fifty years, ever since the loss of your community that had stood on the shores of Bedford Basin for more than 150 years," he said. His voice echoed throughout the gym.

"You lost your houses, your church, all of the places in which you gathered with family and friends to mark the milestones of your lives.

"For all of that, we apologize.

"We apologize to the community elders, including those who did not live to see this day, for the pain and loss of dignity you experienced.

"We apologize to the generations who followed, for the deep wounds you have inherited and the way your lives have been disrupted by the disappearance of your community.

"We apologize for the heartache experienced at the loss of the Seaview United Baptist Church, your spiritual heart of the community, which was removed in the middle of the night. We acknowledge the tremendous importance the church had in your lives, both for the congregation and the community as a whole."

Kelly paused to swallow. He glanced up at the crowd. He looked back at his notes and continued speaking.

"We realize words cannot undo what has been done, but we are profoundly sorry and apologize to each and every one of you and to all the former residents and their descendants.

"The repercussions of what happened in Africville linger to this day. They haunt us in the form of lost opportunities for the young people who were never nurtured in the rich traditions, culture and heritage of Africville.

"They play out in the lingering feelings of hurt and distrust, emotions that this municipality continues to work hard with the African Nova Scotian community to overcome.

"For all these distressing consequences, we apologize."

Kelly paused as the crowd clapped. At the front, Brenda Steed-Ross wept.

"Our history cannot be rewritten but, thankfully, the future is a blank page and, starting today, we hold the pen with which we can write a shared tomorrow. It is in that spirit of respect and reconciliation that we ask your forgiveness," he said.

Loud applause. Tears. Flashbulbs popping. Cameras rolling.

Looking up from his notes, Kelly said, "Let us today start to write the rest of our story together."

Kelly sat down.

Into the silence, that voice. "A public inquiry." Eddie had taken a seat near the front. He was ignored. Eddie's daughter sat with him. Eddie Junior wasn't there, but he had been on CBC Radio the day before. His voice broke as he described watching the protest destroy his father. He said if Eddie Leo Carvery fell, Eddie Leo Carvery II would step up. If he fell, Eddie Leo Carvery III would step up. They'd just keep making Eddie Leo Carverys until they got justice.

More speakers revealed details of compensation, including money to rebuild the church as a memorial to Africville. It would rise again in the vacant land next to the park, just across from Eddie's protest site. An interpretive centre would join it. Training programs. Jobs. Seaview Park would remain as it was, but in the guiding hands of the Africville Heritage Trust Board. The whole area would be once more called Africville.

No individual compensation.

Prayers. Music. Rumblings in the crowd.

More speakers.

Eddie rose from his seat, conferred with a small group of dissenters at the back. He led them on a slow walk up the side of the audience, his fist raised. A small, female police officer asked him to turn back. There were more cops in the crowd. Two vans holding fourteen burly policemen were parked around the corner from the YMCA. Eddie hesitated, walked off to the side. Watched, listened.

Speakers praised Africville, its children and friends: Portia White, Duke Ellington, Louis Armstrong and George Dixon.

Irvine Carvery was called to the podium. He arrived to boos from the back. The front cheered, rose clapping and whistling to drown out the dissenters.

"You know, we have a group at the front here, but there's one chair missing," Irvine said. "I think that my brother Eddie, who has been out in the park protesting, has to be recognized for his efforts."

Irvine was interrupted by a wild burst of cheers. Heads swivelled to find Eddie.

"Eddie has been the visible face of Africville, in Africville. Take my chair, Eddie," Irvine said.

Eddie emerged from the crowd, his face wide open in surprise. He sat in Irvine's seat.

"We, the society, have taken our direction from our elders, from those who were the landowners in Africville. I had the opportunity to speak to Mrs. Howe, Mrs. Mantley, Aunt Emma. It was their wish that we go ahead with our plan," Irvine said to more cheers.

Eddie sat uneasy in the row of suited dignitaries. His left leg jutted out straight, his right was bent, so that he leaned away from the others. He looked to the crowd, to his brother.

"My grandmother said, 'It's not about me. I'm an old woman. It's about the children, the future generations,'" Irvine continued, raising the words of Granny Pink decades after her death. "On behalf of the Africville Genealogy Society, I want to say that today, we close the door on a dark chapter in our history. In closing that door, we open another door for the new beginning of Africville, an Africville that will include everyone. You know, the history of Africville is the history of this city.

"We are going to be so very proud to present that history in a place where my grandchildren, my great-grandchildren, my great-great-grandchildren and future generations beyond that will be able to go to read who we were – who they are. Remember Africville."

Long, loud applause.

Irvine prayed for God to soften the hearts of the dissenters. "When that church is built, Uncle Pa and all the others will have a place where their spirit can rest, and they can finally rest in peace. It's been a long, long battle, but victory is mine."

Irvine sat down next to his older brother as people shouted Amen. More speakers. Eddie rose. Irvine put a hand on his arm. Eddie sat down.

"Let Eddie speak!" a man shouted from the back.

"I've been there for forty years out there on that ground. Let's not get me going," Eddie muttered. "I'm trying to be very nice."

The last speaker sat down. Eddie and Irvine exchanged glances. Eddie walked to the podium. Cheers.

"Before I get carried away and say anything, I just want to thank God for this opportunity," the Hundingo Man said. "I've been laying out there on the ground for ten, twenty years. I've been fighting this fight for Africville for forty years. They were telling me no, Eddie, no – get off the pot. We're not going to be compensated, there will be no nothing, no nothing, no nothing. I've been there on the ground, guys. The City was so good to me, they stole my vehicles, they stole my equipment in the middle of winter. I've had six heart attacks out there on the ground, guys. It's not about Eddie Carvery the villain. Our Lord in heaven, He has a funny sense of humour, because He took a scoundrel like me and He gave me this great opportunity to fight."

Eddie was interrupted by cheers. He choked back tears.

"And you won! And you won!" a woman shouted.

Eddie spoke about the dump, the Infectious Diseases Hospital and the long-term demolition of his community. "They couldn't give us pavement, but they could give us a dump. They couldn't give us sewage, but we had to receive their sewage. We got evicted. It's a vicious cycle of racism, what they did to us in Africville, how we had to survive the winters in Africville. When everybody else had the comforts of their lives and community, we didn't. We were targets for racism. We lived in Africville. What they did to us was outrageous. They created such a state of poverty that by the '60s, when they got ready, well, we were ready to leave, because we didn't know if we could put another winter in that hellhole that they had provided for us when they took our beautiful community – "

He was interrupted by a sour note from the piano.

"I'll go out in a minute," he said to the pianist. Nervous laughter. "You left early. I'm still in Africville. Right today, anybody driving by will see my little caravan of freedom fighters, fighting for what we all should be fighting for. I applaud the City for taking baby steps and recognizing the hard fight Genealogy fought. I applaud Genealogy, but I think our fight has just started. Anyone that agrees with me will come out to Africville and we'll fight for our individual compensation, we'll fight for a public inquiry. Thank you for the apology. Accepted. One down. Two more to go."

Eddie bowed, sat down to loud whoops, whistles and cheers. Irvine greeted him and the two brothers hugged as "A Lament for Africville" was read out.

The piano fired up for real and the band belted out the old hymns that had once echoed through Africville. Eddie danced, swinging his arms and singing, pausing to shake hands as people lined up to congratulate him. Closing prayers. More tears. Eddie was swallowed up in a media scrum.

When the meeting ended, the media, politicians, Africvillians and the descendents of Africvillians trickled out into the windy North End streets of Halifax, humming, heading back to work, heading home.

Eddie headed home and to work. He went back to Africville.

Afterword

It's been two days since the extraordinary events which closed this book. A howling wind is driving a monsoon rain through Halifax. I've just returned from visiting Eddie in Africville. He's in a quiet, peaceful mood, slowly digesting the apology and the recognition of his protest. It's not a complete victory – he still wants a public inquiry and individual compensation – but it is a victory. After forty lonely years of defeat, that takes some adjusting. At the end of the apology ceremony, Eddie went home and threw up. But he seems happy today.

The church is coming back, along with an interpretive centre. The roots of his ancestors are bursting through the ground and reclaiming the land. Eddie's wondering about this new future of his, of Africville's.

"That church is going to need a curator," he muses. "I could do that."

Fair enough. He's been the eternal flame burning in Africville through its darkest hours and wildest storms. He'd make a great custodian.

"I'm not afraid of moving on," he told me before catching a ride into the city to visit his children. That's a priority for him, now – to try to make up for lost time with his family. I've met some of his children and they all adore their father.

Eddie's only worry about this book is that it might bring fresh pain to those he's hurt before. The whole book can be considered his apology to them, he said.

I first encountered Eddie in August 2009. I was reporting on the annual Africville summer reunion and went to Seaview Park in search of a few quotes about how nice it was that the City had renamed the service road "Africville Road." Instead, I found Eddie Carvery. He spoke for forty-five minutes, delivering a powerful oration on the history of Africville, the crime that was committed against it, and his unending fight for freedom. I was blown away and returned two days later to propose we collaborate on a book about his life. He agreed on the spot and we got to work. I spent the rest of the summer and the fall visiting Eddie in Africville and interviewed him for an hour or two a day, four or five days a week, as our schedules permitted. Those interviews, perhaps totalling forty hours, formed the bulk of this biography.

I read every book on Africville I could find. That included *The Africville Relocation Report* by Donald Clairmont and Dennis Magill, *The Spirit of Africville* by the Africville Genealogical Society and *Razing Africville: A Geography of Racism* by Jennifer Nelson. Also exceptionally helpful was the National Film Board of Canada's *Remember Africville*, directed by Shelagh MacKenzie, and the archives of the Halifax Public Library. Most of the newspaper reports cited in this book come from their clippings of *The Chronicle-Herald* and the Halifax *Daily News*.

The chapters on Victor Carvery, Eddie's steadfast lieutenant in the protest, come from a series of interviews I conducted with Victor in the fall of 2009. The sections on Irvine Carvery are based on several interviews I conducted with him over the same period. Two of Eddie's former partners, Stephanie Sparks and Dawn, provided important recollections of events and unique perspectives on Eddie and his protest.

I interviewed many journalism colleagues for their recollections of the high-profile period when the G7 came to Eddie's protest in 1995. The CBC's online archives of video and sound recordings from the period of Africville's destruction were especially valuable, as was the Africville exhibit at the Black Cultural Centre outside of Dartmouth.

The account of the Black Panther visit to Halifax was provided to me by Rocky Jones, who generously took time out of his very busy schedule, which includes writing his own memoir, to fill me in. Robert Ashe's biography of Dave Downey, *Halifax Champion: Black Power in Gloves*, added further detail. I was present when the park warden hassled Eddie and for the other events depicted from 2009 to 2010. Some names have been changed and it is possible that some of the chronology of Eddie's life is incorrect. If any mistakes are brought to my attention, I will post corrections on my website. You can reach me at jon@jontattrie.ca.

The Hermit of Africville originally stopped at Chapter 73. My publisher liked it, but wanted more for the ending. I was covering an anti-racism march in Halifax later that day when BlackBerrys started buzzing and word got out that the mayor was going to apologize to Africville. I had my new ending.

I interviewed Irvine Carvery for a newspaper article shortly before the apology was delivered. He said that in the past, he'd been described as optimistic that the church would be rebuilt and compensation paid. This time, he told me, he was confident it would happen.

I hope that confidence is justified and that as you are reading these words, the church is being rebuilt or is rebuilt. Perhaps you bought this book from its gift shop and noticed an elderly custodian with Einstein hair showing people around Africville. After centuries of breaking promises, I hope my city has finally honoured its word and done the right thing.

To see more photographs and videos of Eddie Carvery and his family, visit my website, www.jontattrie.ca. Eddie doesn't have e-mail, but if you send a message to me, I'll make sure he gets it. If you're in Halifax, drive out past where the pavement ends, where the Hermit of Africville lives, and stop by to say hello.

Jon Tattrie
Halifax, Nova Scotia
February 2010